HOW TO REPRESENT YOURSELF IN COURT:

Litigation advice for those who cannot afford an attorney

Jay Barr

(c) 2019, lawsuitforms.org. All rights reserved. This guide and any portion thereof may only be used by the single person it was purchased for. Republishing, sharing, or otherwise reproducing any portion of this guide for any other use is strictly prohibited, except as expressly authorized by Federal law, the author, amazon.com, and/or the publisher.

Table of Contents

INTRODUCTION: Overview of Civil Litigation 1

CHAPTER 1: Filing a Civil Complaint 19

CHAPTER 2: Serving the Complaint 27

CHAPTER 3: Filing an Answer to the Complaint 33

CHAPTER 4: Pretrial Motion Practice 37

CHAPTER 5: The Discovery Process...47

CHAPTER 6: How to Find and Prepare Evidence...........................61

CHAPTER 7: Arbitration 71

CHAPTER 8: Jury Trials 75

CHAPTER 9: At the Hearing 81

CHAPTER 10: How to Collect on A Judgment.................................95

CONCLUSION 101

APPENDIX 1: Sample Pleadings 103

APPENDIX 2: Glossary 125

INTRODUCTION:
Overview of Civil Litigation

Thank you for purchasing 'How to Represent Yourself in Court' from lawsuitforms.org! If you are involved in any kind of civil litigation, this guide will serve you well. While it is always advisable to have a competent attorney advocating for your interests, we recognize the simple fact that not everyone can afford to hire an attorney when they need legal assistance.

This guide will be of immense help to those who need legal advice, but are unable to retain counsel. It contains detailed information on each step of the civil legal process. Use this guide if you have been sued, are thinking of suing someone (or have already done so), or if you just want more information on how the United States civil court system works.

This guide contains information on all aspects of civil litigation, including:

1. How to draft a summons and complaint if you need to sue someone;

2. How to write and file an answer if you have been served with a complaint;

3. How to engage in the discovery process and acquire evidence/testimony from the opposing party;

4. What evidence you will need to prove your claims or defenses in front of a judge or jury (and how to obtain it);

5. How to file and/or respond to some of the most common motions you will encounter in a civil lawsuit;

6. How to introduce evidence, question witnesses, and offer objections at trial or arbitration;

7. How to collect on a judgment via the garnishment of wages and/or bank accounts.

Each chapter is presented in an approximately chronological, easy to follow order, covering the entire litigation process, from filing a complaint all the way through arbitration/trial.[1] It also includes an easy to understand glossary of the most common legal terms you will encounter. However, before we dive into the details of a civil lawsuit, here are a few key points to keep in mind:

- All of our guides are created by licensed attorneys with years of experience and are written in a straightforward, easy to understand manner with a minimum of legal jargon. Sample documents are included in Appendix 1, but keep in mind that there are for one particular state and the form of the documents in your state may vary.

- Civil court procedure varies from state to state! Most (if not all) of the concepts contained in this guide will certainly apply in

---

[1] This guide does not cover the appeals process.

most other states, but be aware that the exact procedure may be different (how to find the specific rules of each state is discussed below).

- This guide is intentionally written in an easy to understand format that can be used by anyone in the United States (or anyone who wants to learn about the legal system in the United States). It endeavors to avoid legal jargon and simplify the issues whenever possible. Be aware that legal terms may have different names in different states, but refer to the same thing. The purpose of this guide is to offer an easy to understand process for navigating the legal system, rather than offering a detailed review of every possible scenario and legal term that may be encountered in court.

- Legal jargon and obtuse rules often make the legal process seem much more complicated than it really is. Law is not rocket science or brain surgery and you will be surprised at just how much of the legal field is based on simple, common-sense theories, even when the rules seem to be written in a different language. After reading this guide you will be able to navigate this needlessly complicated arena with confidence.

Key Points About Civil Litigation

If you are (or might become) a plaintiff or defendant in a civil lawsuit, you need to know the basics of how the civil legal system works:

- Almost every civil lawsuit in any state is filed in that state's trial court system. These courts are usually organized by county. The exact name of this court will vary from state to state. For example, in Oregon the trial court system is referred to as Oregon Circuit Court, in California it is called California Superior Court, and in Texas, it is referred to as Texas District Court.

- The federal government also has their own court system, referred to as United States District Court. The vast majority of civil cases will be heard in a state, rather than federal, court, but the principles in this guide will generally apply to both court systems.

- Every state has hundreds of laws (often referred to as 'statutes'), which will all have similar, but slightly different names, such as the Oregon Revised Statutes or California Code. In addition to statutes, states will have specific rules of civil procedure that all courts must follow. They may also have trial court rules that further detail the procedures that govern civil actions.

- In order to track down all these laws and rules in your state, keep in mind the following:

- Statutes are created by the state legislature and you will easily be able to find the official codes online by going to your state legislature's website. The rules of civil procedure should also be available at the state level.

- To find out about your trial court rules, contact the specific courthouse your case is (or will be) heard in. You can also contact the state trial court administration website.

- Finally, don't forget to inquire about whether or not your specific courthouse has supplementary local rules that are only followed in that specific court.

- Although this may sound daunting, do not be intimidated! You will not need to read every statute and rule of civil procedure in order to competently represent yourself. In fact, once you know the specific legal issue you need to look into, you will easily be able to find the relevant information, whether it is a statute, state-wide trial court rule, or a local rule.

- Besides statutes and rules, United States civil law is also based on court precedent, meaning that anytime a judge is deciding an issue regarding your case, they will look to similar cases heard in that state's appellate courts and supreme court to help them decide how to rule. Such prior cases are considered binding authority and the trial court judge will be bound to make a decision that does not conflict with prior case law. Proper review and analysis of case law is beyond the scope of this guide (and beyond more than a few attorneys!), but you do need to be aware that such references may come up in your case. If you do need to review a particular case, your local law librarian will be able to show you how to access a database containing most cases that are cited in any proceeding.

- In addition to reviewing laws online, your local law library will be a great resource for more in-depth research. Check with your particular county court to find out the hours and location of your local law library.

- Most civil claims need to be proven by a PREPONDERANCE OF THE EVIDENCE, which simply means that the claims made by the plaintiff must be 'more likely than not' to have occurred. The burden of proof is always on the plaintiff. They need to introduce evidence related to each element of their claim that will show the judge it is 'more likely than not' to be the truth. If the plaintiff fails to do so, the defendant will win the case, regardless of whether or not they put on any kind of defense.

- One of the best ways to learn about the civil process is to go to the courthouse and watch a few hearings or trials. Contact the calendaring department of your local courthouse and find out when and what types of civil hearings/trials are being held. These proceedings are open to the public and anyone can attend. Just make sure you are quiet and respectful when watching any court proceeding.

Steps in a Civil Lawsuit

Generally speaking, all civil lawsuits contain the following steps (which will be discussed in greater detail throughout this guide):

1. A COMPLAINT is filed by the PLAINTIFF;

2. A SUMMONS is issued and it is served on the DEFENDANT along with a copy of the complaint.

3. The Defendant then has to respond to the complaint by filing an ANSWER or MOTION. The Defendant will usually have 20-30 days from the date they receive the summons to respond.

4. Some states require the parties to engage in mandatory arbitration in certain circumstances (such as when the damages claimed are less than $50,000). If your case is subject to arbitration, an arbitrator will be assigned

relatively early in the process (see Chapter 7 for more information on arbitration).

5. If an Answer is filed, both sides then engage in DISCOVERY;

6. Discovery, generally speaking, includes the following:

    a. Exchange of any and all documents that are relevant to proving or disproving any claim or defense by submitting a REQUEST FOR PRODUCTION to the opposing party;

    b. Conducting DEPOSITIONS, where the parties and/or witnesses testify under oath and everything is transcribed by a court reporter.

    c. Sending INTERROGATORIES to the opposing party, which is a list of written questions that the opposing party is required to answer.

    d. Obtaining testimony and other evidence from third parties via subpoenas and depositions.

7. After discovery is complete, it is possible that the SUMMARY JUDGMENT process may begin. Summary Judgment is a process in which either side may try to get a ruling in their favor without proceeding to trial or arbitration. Summary Judgment is sought when there are no genuine issues of fact to be decided at trial. When the facts are not in dispute and the only issues are legal in nature, a judge may grant summary judgment in favor of one party, without conducting a full trial.

8. If Summary Judgment does not take place, the case will proceed to TRIAL or arbitration.

9. After trial, the losing side may file an APPEAL if certain conditions are met. A review of the appeals process is beyond the scope of this guide, but if you are sure you have good cause to appeal, you will need to file your appeal (or at least notice of your appeal) within a certain time after the judgment is entered into the court record (often, 30 days).

10. After trial, the prevailing party will most likely engage in collection efforts, often by garnishing wages and/or bank accounts.

That's it! That's all there is to the legal process. Of course, the details can get a bit more complicated, but this is the course almost every single civil lawsuit will take. If this process makes sense to you, you will easily be able to understand the rest of this guide.

Glossary of Terms

The following glossary contains definitions of some of the most common legal terms you are likely to encounter in civil court. You should review the glossary now before proceeding. Keep in mind that some of the terms below might not be relevant to your particular case. Also, note that the definitions in this glossary reflect how the terms are used in this guide in relation to civil court proceedings. Other legal definitions of the same terms may vary slightly or be somewhat more detailed. These terms also may vary somewhat from state to state. The glossary below is grouped in an easy to follow, non-alphabetical order that reflects how a case would generally proceed. An alphabetical glossary of the same terms is included in Appendix 2.

In the Beginning:

PARTY: A plaintiff or defendant in a civil case.

PLAINTIFF: A person who files a civil lawsuit against a defendant.

DEFENDANT: A person who has been accused of wrongdoing in civil court in the form of a complaint being filed against them.

PRO SE: Latin phrase meaning, "for oneself". It refers to any plaintiff or defendant that does not have an attorney. They are referred to as a *pro se* litigant or proceeding *pro se*.

CONTRACT LAW: One of two broad categories of civil lawsuits. All legal issues dealing with any written or oral agreement will be based on contract law.

TORT LAW: The other broad category of civil lawsuits that basically includes any type of wrongful act committed by another (other than breach of contract cases), such as battery or negligence.

PLEADING (noun): Any formal document that is filed with the court in a civil case.

SUMMONS: A command to appear and defend oneself in a civil lawsuit. Served with a complaint. Failure to appear can result in a default judgment being entered against the defendant.

COMPLAINT: The initial document filed by a plaintiff that begins a civil lawsuit. It is a statement of how the plaintiff has been wronged by the defendant, why they should be compensated, and how much compensation they believe is warranted. It includes one or more claims for relief and alleges how each element of that claim has been satisfied.

CLAIM FOR RELIEF: A specific cause of action alleged in a complaint, such as a claim of negligence or a claim of racial discrimination.

ELEMENT: A specific aspect of a claim that must be properly alleged (and ultimately proven) to prevail on a claim for relief. A claim will normally have several elements, each of which must be proven by a preponderance of the evidence.

ANSWER: The formal reply to a complaint, filed by the defendant. An answer will usually deny the claims made in the complaint and/or will otherwise assert how the plaintiff is not entitled to any of the relief sought.

AFFIRMATIVE DEFENSE: A type of defense asserted in a defendant's answer in which, even if the allegations in the plaintiff's complaint are true, the plaintiff is still not entitled to relief. For example, if the allegations in the complaint are true, but the statute of limitations has expired, the defendant would assert the affirmative defense of failure to bring a claim within the statutory period.

STATUTE OF LIMITATIONS: A period set by law in which a claim for relief must be filed. For example, if the statute of limitations on a personal injury (negligence) case is two years, the plaintiff would need to file a claim for negligence within two years of the date they discovered the injury.

CONTRACT: Any agreement (oral or written), in which an offer has been made by one party, accepted by another, and some consideration has been given (such as money, or performance of a specific task). Breach of contract is one of the most commonly filed civil claims.

Procedural Issues:

STATUTES: The codified laws of a state. The official name of these statutes will vary from state to state.

RULES OF CIVIL PROCEDURE: The basic rules of civil court proceedings. Each state will have their own set of civil procedure rules (the official name of these rules will vary from state to state).

TRIAL COURT RULES: More specific rules of a state that govern courtroom procedure which all county courts must follow.

LOCAL RULES: Specific rules put in place by county courts. All proceedings in these particular counties must follow their local rules.

SMALL CLAIMS COURT: A division of a state court that handles claims of low economic value (the exact amount varies by state). In most states, attorneys are not allowed to represent parties in small claims court. It is intended to be a less formal and more cost-effective venue for resolving civil disputes.

SERVICE: The term used to refer to specific notice that pleadings have been received by an opposing party.

PROCESS SERVER: A person who is hired by a party to deliver legal documents to persons in accordance with the rules of civil procedure.

CERTIFICATE OF SERVICE: A document filed with the court (signed by the process server) showing that service has been completed in accordance with the rules of civil procedure.

DEFAULT JUDGMENT: A judgment entered against a defendant who has failed to appear after being properly served with a summons and complaint.

MEDIATION: A formal meeting between the parties and a neutral mediator in which the mediator attempts to broker a settlement that is agreeable to both sides. Unlike an arbitrator, the mediator does not have any authority to issue a decision in favor of one party. Their only purpose is to negotiate with both parties and attempt to craft a mutually agreeable settlement. In some instances, parties are required to attend a mediation session and work towards resolving the issue in good faith.

ARBITRATION: A less formal, but usually binding, proceeding in which a civil dispute is resolved by a private arbitrator, rather than a judge. In some cases, arbitration is mandatory.

CONTEMPT OF COURT: The offense of disobeying a court order. A judge can find a person in contempt and impose sanctions (usually a fine or other civil penalty, but on rare occasions it can include incarceration). In addition, if a party believes someone else is disobeying an order, they can ask the judge to find that person in contempt by filing a motion.

HEARING: A proceeding before a judge in which evidence is presented and a decision is made. The decision at a hearing may affect one aspect of a case, or it may resolve the case entirely, depending on the nature of the specific hearing.

TRIAL: A proceeding in which a final decision is made based on the merits of a case. A hearing where evidence is presented and a judge or jury finds in favor of the plaintiff or defendant.

BENCH TRIAL: A trial in which there is no jury. The judge will decide all issues of law and fact.

JURY TRIAL: A trial in which a jury decides all factual issues. A judge will preside over the case and decide all legal issues, but the final decision regarding liability and damages will be made by the jury.

JUDGMENT CREDITOR: A person who has been awarded monetary damages in a civil lawsuit.

JUDGMENT DEBTOR: A person who has been ordered to pay monetary damages in a civil lawsuit.

APPEAL: A request for a higher court to review the decision of a lower court. Appeals are not allowed in every instance. There must be a specific reason (specified by the courts or state law) that allows an appeal. For example, if a judge excludes evidence and you object, you could appeal, asking for a new trial. But if a jury simply decides against you because they found the other party more convincing, you generally cannot appeal.

GARNISHMENT: The legal seizing of another person's property (such as wages or funds in a bank account). Garnishment is often instituted to collect money awarded in a judgment.

Motions Practice:

MOTION: Any formal request by a party, asking the court to take a certain course of action.

RESPONSE: A response to a motion filed by the opposing party.

REPLY: A reply to a party's response to a motion (filed by the party who originally filed the motion).

DECLARATION: A written statement made under oath, usually attached to a motion or other pleading to support the arguments contained therein. A declaration can be made by a party or anyone else who has personal knowledge that is relevant to the case.

MOTION TO DISMISS: A formal request by a defendant to dismiss one or more of plaintiff's claims. Usually due to the plaintiff failing to properly allege a cause of action.

DISMISSAL WITHOUT PREJUDICE: The dismissal of a plaintiff's case wherein they can refile their complaint. In other words, a judge thought the case had serious flaws, but the flaws could potentially be resolved and the case could still be refiled if the deficiencies are corrected.

DISMISSAL WITH PREJUDICE: The dismissal of a plaintiff's case, wherein the plaintiff cannot refile against the defendant regarding the same issue. The judge has decided that the problems with the case are so great, they cannot possibly be corrected.

MOTION FOR SUMMARY JUDGMENT: A formal request by either party asking the judge to find in their favor without going to trial/ arbitration. A party files a motion for summary judgment when they believe there are no material issues of fact that need to be considered in a trial/ arbitration. For example, if a plaintiff in a deposition admits that a specific element of a claim never actually occurred, the defendant may move for summary judgment because there is no dispute about the existence of that specific element of the claim.

MOTION TO COMPEL: A formal request by either party to force the other party to produce certain documents or answer certain questions. Such a motion would be filed after a party asks for the information, but the other side has refused to provide it. At this point the party ordered to produce the information can be found in contempt if the motion is granted and they still refuse to produce the documents or answer the questions.

ORAL ARGUMENT: Appearances by both parties (usually in relation to a filed motion) to argue their points personally in front of a judge before the judge makes a decision regarding the motion. Oral argument is held after a motion, response, and reply have all been filed.

Evidence and Discovery:

EVIDENCE: Anything that is submitted in a court proceeding to prove or disprove any claim or defense. Evidence includes (but is not limited to) oral testimony of witnesses, documents, video recordings, and material objects.

DISCOVERY: The stage of a civil lawsuit wherein both parties are obligated to turn over any potential evidence that is relevant to a claim or defense.

PREJUDICIAL: In this context, prejudicial refers to how *unfairly* harmful a piece of evidence is. Evidence that would not be excluded for any other reason, can still be excluded if it will unfairly bias a jury. For example, if the jury knows a party has been convicted of a crime unrelated to the issue at hand, that could unfairly skew their impression of the party. The party could seek to have that fact excluded as having more prejudicial than probative value.

PROBATIVE: A term used to describe how strong a piece of evidence is in regards to its ability to help prove or disprove any claim or defense. How probative a piece of evidence is will often be a factor in whether or not it is admitted into the record. Evidence that has no probative value will likely be excluded.

REQUEST FOR ADMISSIONS (RFA): A formal request issued by a party during discovery in which they ask the opposing party to admit or deny specific facts about the case.

REQUEST FOR PRODUCTION (RFP): A formal request issued by a party during discovery in which they ask for all potential evidence (usually in the form of written documents) that is relevant to any claim or defense in a civil case.

INTERROGATORIES: A formal request issued by a party during discovery in which they ask the other party to answer a list of questions in writing.

DEPOSITION: A formal interview of a witness that is recorded (usually by a court reporter transcribing the deposition).

DEPONENT: The witness who is being deposed.

WITNESS: Any person that provides testimony in a court proceeding. They can be a party to the litigation or any other person.

SUBPOENA: A command by a court or attorney requiring a person to appear for a deposition or hearing/trial/arbitration.

SUBPOENA DUCES TECUM: A command by a court or attorney requiring a person to produce specific documents or other material objects.

EXHIBIT: Any piece of evidence (other than witness testimony) that is submitted for review in a court proceeding, whether at trial/arbitration or pursuant to a motion, deposition or other hearing.

OBJECTION: A formal protest by one party to the actions of the other party. For example, if a party seeks to submit evidence that is not in accordance with a state's rules of evidence, a party might object to its entry on the grounds that it fails to comply with the said rule. Alternatively, if a party tries to ask a witness a question, the answer to which would not be admissible, the opposing party should object to the question before the witness answers.

Now that you have a basic understanding of the civil court system, we can proceed to Chapter 1, wherein you will learn how to prepare and file a complaint. Chapter 2 will instruct you on how to properly serve the complaint and Chapter 3 details how to respond to a complaint by filing an answer. Congratulations! You are well on your way to having a firm grasp of the civil litigation process. . .

CHAPTER 1:
Filing a Civil Complaint

Now that you understand the basics of the civil legal system, the next step is to learn about the initial pleading in any civil case: The complaint.

Drafting the Complaint

If you think someone has wronged you and you are entitled to compensation, you may have no choice but to file a civil lawsuit. Of course, it would be nice if you could politely ask the person to pay for all the damage they have caused, but unfortunately, things rarely work that way.

However, before you can write a complaint, you must be sure that you have a valid claim. You cannot just allege you were wronged and expect a court to award you damages. You must be able to categorize your lawsuit into a specific claim, such as negligence or breach of contract. Then, you must allege each specific element of the claim in your complaint. If you can ultimately prove those allegations, you will likely prevail at trial.

A discussion of every single civil claim and their individual elements is beyond the scope of this guide, but here is brief overview of some of the most common claims filed in civil court and their basic elements.

NOTE: The exact elements of a claim will vary from state to state! It is imperative that you make sure to check the specific elements of your claim in your state!!!

1. Breach of Contract. **Generally speaking**, the plaintiff must allege and ultimately prove:

    a. Existence of a contract (either oral or written[2]), which includes an offer, acceptance, and some sort of consideration (such as money paid for a task performed).

    b. Breach of said contract by the Defendant.

    c. Damages incurred.

2. Negligence. **Generally speaking**, the plaintiff must allege and ultimately prove:

    a. The defendant's conduct caused the plaintiff harm;

    b. The risk of that harm was foreseeable;

    c. That defendant's conduct was unreasonable in light of the risk;

---

[2] Contrary to popular belief, most oral contracts are usually enforceable in most states. The specific terms of the contact are just harder to prove.

d. The harm caused by the defendant resulted in the plaintiff incurring damages.

3. Battery. ***Generally speaking*** the plaintiff must allege and ultimately prove:

    a. The defendant intended to cause harmful or offensive physical contact;

    b. Such contact actually occurred;

    c. The plaintiff suffered damages (either economic or non-economic) as a result of such contact.

4. Theft (called 'conversion' in legalese). ***Generally speaking***, the plaintiff must allege and ultimately prove:

    a. The defendant exercised dominion and control over the plaintiff's property to such an extent that the defendant should be ordered to return the property or pay the plaintiff its full value, in addition to compensating the plaintiff for loss of use of the property. If the loss of the property was only temporary and the plaintiff got it back, they can still claim damages for loss of use.

Additional Considerations:

In addition to making sure you have a valid claim before you file a complaint, you also need to be aware that sometimes a state will have specific rules that may apply to your case. For example:

- If you are suing any type of government body in state court, it is likely that you may have to file a Tort Claim Notice before you can file your lawsuit. The time to file a tort claim notice in most states is much shorter than the normal statute of limitations (although once you file the notice, you will then have the rest of the statute of limitations period to file your claim).

- If you are suing a contractor for work done on your home, you may have to give them proper notice of your intent to file a lawsuit before you actually file a complaint.

- If you have a written contract with someone, you must check the terms of the contract and make sure you have not agreed to a mandatory private arbitration program. If you have, you will be required to go through that process instead of (or at least before) filing in civil court. In that event, this guide will still be quite useful, as any such arbitration will almost certainly involve discovery, evidence, and witness testimony, the processes of which will be based on state law.

Once you have reviewed the pre-filing requirements in your state and you feel you have good cause, you can start drafting a complaint. Samples of a completed complaint from the State of Oregon are included in Appendix 1 of this guide, but keep in mind that the proper formatting will vary from state to state. Review your state's trial court rules to find the proper formatting guidelines. It is always a good idea to make sure that your pleadings are professional looking and on par with what would be filed by an attorney. That said, if you are representing yourself, most courts will not be too concerned about whether or not you are in strict compliance with the formatting rules (also, if you are reading this guide in ebook format, be aware that the formatting of the samples may be somewhat skewed). As long as your complaint is easy to read and your claims are laid out clearly and concisely, the court clerk will almost certainly accept your pleading.

The Structure of the Complaint

Once the proper formatting is in place, you will need to write the body of your complaint. Most civil complaints will have the following structure:

1. A simple, introductory sentence. This will almost always be, "Plaintiff brings this Complaint against Defendant and alleges as follows:".

2. A statement of jurisdiction. Each complaint should state the allegations that will inform the court why bringing the action in this particular courthouse is proper (it will usually be because the defendant resides there and/or the actions giving rise to the complaint took place in that particular jurisdiction. Note that plaintiffs generally cannot sue in the court that is most convenient to them.

3. Paragraphs alleging facts that (if proven) satisfy all the elements of your claims. It is important to remember that you do not need to try and prove your allegations in the complaint. You only need to make the allegation. Proving what happened will take place at trial.

4. Claims for relief. This is where you spell out each cause of action you have against the defendant. Most complaints will only have 1-3 claims for relief, but more than that is not too unusual.

5. Prayer for relief. This is where you spell out exactly what you want the court to award you. It primarily consists of asking for economic and/or non-economic monetary damages, and an award of the expenses you incurred as a result of filing the complaint (such as filing and service fees).

Claims for Relief and the Prayer for Relief:

Once facts supporting the elements of each claim are alleged in the body of your complaint, you need to make a claim for relief for each cause of action and state how the defendant's actions have caused you damages. For example, your first claim for relief might look like this:

First Claim for Relief (Breach of contract):

10.

The actions of Defendant described above constitute a material breach of the contract between the parties. Defendant's actions have caused Plaintiff to incur $20,000 in economic damages.

You would then go on to your second claim for relief, and so on.
Finally, in the prayer for relief, you will state the total amount of damages you want the court to award, request your expenses (referred to as costs and disbursements in legal jargon), and request interest on any award. Most states have a statutorily set interest rate for judgments awarded in a civil case.

Where to File the Complaint:

When filing a complaint, you need to make sure that it is filed in the proper courthouse that has the appropriate authority to hear your case (referred to as venue). For most civil claims, proper venue can be either of the following:

1. The county where the defendant resides; or,

2. The county where the events that are the subject of the complaint occurred.

Many times, these will both be the same county. If they are not, it is generally best to file suit in the county where the defendant resides, as this will avoid any potential arguments about which venue is proper.

Once you have drafted your complaint, you will need to file it at the courthouse and pay the applicable filing fee. Most *pro se* litigants prefer to file documents in person at the courthouse's civil filing window. However, many state courts now have electronic filing capability. Check with your local courthouse to find out if you can file documents online and be aware that you may have to pay an application fee to gain access to the online system.

Also, if you have limited financial means, you may be able to qualify for a fee waiver/deferral, but the standard for approval is generally quite high. If you think you may be approved, ask the court clerk for a fee waiver application. Next, you will have to draft a summons (or acquire one from the court) and serve it on the defendant with a copy of the complaint, which is the subject of Chapter 2.

If you follow the guidelines in this chapter, you will have a professional looking complaint that is on par with anything submitted by an attorney. If you can draft a complaint, you can easily draft most other civil pleadings as well!

CHAPTER 2:
Serving the Complaint

Once your complaint is filed with the courthouse you will need to serve it on the defendant. Rules regarding service are very specific and they must be followed precisely! Although there are a few different ways to serve a defendant, the best course of action is to have the summons and complaint served personally by an independent process server or your local sheriff. This way, there will be no doubt that the person was actually served (see below for more details on process servers).

Step One: Draft or obtain a Summons

Before you serve your complaint, you may need to draft a summons. A summons is the official document that puts the defendant on notice that a lawsuit has been filed against them. It also gives instructions on how to appear and answer the complaint. Without a summons, your complaint is just a list of demands without any legal authority, even if it has been filed at the courthouse.

Some states (such as California) have mandatory summons forms that must be used, some states may have optional forms you can use, and some states may require you to draft the summons yourself. Fortunately, the summons is mostly boilerplate and is easy to fill out. A sample of a summons from Oregon is included in Appendix 1, but as with other forms, the exact language that you will need in your state will vary. ***The format of the summons in this guide should not be considered valid for any other state besides Oregon!*** Check your state's rules of civil procedure for the legal requirements for issuing a summons and completing service.

Step Two: How to Find the Defendant

Ideally, you will already know where the defendant resides or does business, so finding the proper address for service won't be a problem. If you are serving the defendant personally, you might not even need their address (so long as you know where they are going to be on any given day). If, however, you do not know the defendant's address, use the following resources:

Court Records:

Most courthouses (or the nearest law library) will have a computer terminal where you can look up all civil and criminal records in the state. If the defendant has been sued before or has been charged with a crime, their address will likely be included in the court records. Just keep in mind that proper spelling is important, the address information may be outdated (especially if the only record is several years old), and there could very well be someone with the same name as the person you are looking for (try to use birthdate information to confirm, if you have that available).

Motor Vehicle Records:

Many state motor vehicle departments allow process servers and members of the public to access certain information. You may be able to obtain a defendant's address this way, but you will have to check with your state department to inquire about what information can be released.

Business Records:

All individuals and companies doing business in a state usually have to register with some sort of state agency. As part of this registration, they are usually required to list a 'Registered Agent', which is an entity or person that is designated to accept mail and legal documents on behalf of a business. For larger corporations, separate companies are used who do nothing but act as a registered agent for many different businesses. If you are suing a business, all legal documents should be sent to the registered agent, rather than the business's headquarters. Check your state's business registry for this information.

Step Three: How to Serve the Summons and Complaint

Once you know the defendant's address, you can serve them in a variety of ways. However, as mentioned above, personal service by a professional process server or the local sheriff is the best option. If you feel another method of service is appropriate for your case, you will need to check your state's rules of civil procedure for alternative methods of service.

Personal Service:

Personal service, as the name implies, means serving the defendant directly. It is usually the best course of action. Having a neutral, third-party serve a defendant directly greatly reduces the chance that the defendant will claim they were never served properly.

The best way to have a person/business served is to hire a professional process server. Of course, this is also the most expensive and the cost for such service is usually between $50-60. However, it is often worthwhile as this price will include a few attempts at one specific address and you can also rely on their professional expertise when it comes to making sure service is completed effectively. A simple internet search will give you a list of the process servers working in your geographic area.

The second-best option (and usually the second most expensive) is to pay a sheriff's deputy to serve the documents. Sheriff's departments in most states provide this service to the public for a fee.

If you do not want to incur the expense of hiring a professional process server, any adult of sound mind and body who is a resident of your state should be able to serve a defendant (but check your local laws). You can even go with the person, so long as you are not the one who actually gives the documents to the defendant. The server simply needs to identify the defendant, inform the defendant that the server has some documents for him/her, and hand them over. That's it. You don't need to explain who you are or the nature of the documents.

If the person refuses to take them, simply inform them that it is really in their best interest to accept these documents and leave them at their feet (or on a counter/table/etc).

Step Four: Filing the Proof of Service

Once service has been completed, the person who served the documents needs to sign a CERTIFICATE OF SERVICE, which is then filed with the courthouse to prove that the defendant has been made aware of the pending lawsuit. If you used a professional process server or the sheriff's department, they *should* fill out their own form and send it to the courthouse themselves (but follow up to make sure they do not forget).

Once service has been completed, the defendant will have a certain number of days from the date of service to file an answer (usually 30 days). If the defendant has not filed an answer or motion within the allotted time after being served you will need to petition the court for a default judgment. This usually involves filing a motion with the court, informing them that the defendant has failed to appear and asking the court to enter a judgment in your favor.

Serving Other Pleadings:

Once the defendant has been served with the summons and complaint, the rules regarding service of other legal documents are much more relaxed. If the defendant is represented by an attorney, you should be able to mail all further pleadings to them via first class mail. If the defendant is not represented, you should send the pleadings via first class mail to the Defendant's last known address (presumably where they were served with the summons and complaint) or the address they listed in their answer. Also, remember to fill out a certificate of service for each group of documents you send going forward.

If the defendant has been properly served with a summons and complaint and filed an answer, you will need to begin the discovery process, which is the subject of Chapter 5. If the defendant has filed a motion before filing an answer, Chapter 4 will tell you how to respond. Also, refer to the 'Summary Judgment' section of Chapter 4, if the opposing party files a motion for summary judgment at any point after the initial pleadings have been filed (this would most likely happen after discovery is completed).

CHAPTER 3:
Filing an Answer to the Complaint

If you have been sued for any reason, you will have received a summons and complaint detailing the specifics of the allegations. ***IT IS IMPERATIVE THAT YOU DO NOT IGNORE THE SUMMONS AND COMPLAINT!!!*** You must file an answer (or in some cases a motion) within the time indicated in the summons! If you fail to do so, a default judgment will likely be entered against you and you will be forced to pay the plaintiff all of the damages they alleged in their complaint, regardless of whether or not they are accurate.

Writing the Answer

A sample answer from the state of Oregon is included in Appendix 1 and answer form packets for several states are available for purchase at www.lawsuitforms.org. As with the complaint, following your court's formatting guidelines is always a good idea, but it is more important to ensure that your answer is clear and concise. An answer primarily consists of simply admitting or denying each allegation in the plaintiff's complaint (although some states allow a defendant to make a simple, general denial of all of Plaintiff's claims).

Admissions and Denials:

The main body of the answer should address each specific paragraph of the complaint and state whether the defendant ADMITS or DENIES the allegations in each paragraph. A typical response would look like this: "Defendant DENIES the allegations in paragraph 4 of the Complaint." Generally, you should admit any minor fact that is easily proven and not in dispute (such as a jurisdictional allegation alleging you live in a certain county). However, if there is any doubt, it is always best to err on the side of caution and deny the allegation. Never rely on your memory when responding to a complaint. Even if you are pretty sure the allegation is true, simply state something similar to: "Defendant does not have sufficient knowledge to admit or deny the allegations in Paragraph 6 of the Complaint; they are therefore DENIED".

Often, a portion of a complaint's paragraph will have allegations that can be safely admitted, but other portions that should be denied. In such instance, state something similar to: "In regards to Paragraph 3 of the Complaint, Defendant ADMITS that Plaintiff gave him $20,000, but DENIES the remaining allegations." In addition, if there are a string of paragraphs in the complaint that you are admitting or denying, you can usually group them all in a single sentence like this: "Defendant DENIES the allegations in Paragraphs 7-10 of the Complaint."

Affirmative Defenses:

After you have admitted or denied each paragraph of the complaint, you should allege any AFFIRMATIVE DEFENSES you may have. An affirmative defense is a defense that does not depend on the veracity of the plaintiff's allegations. In other words, even if everything the plaintiff alleges in the complaint is true, they are still not entitled to relief. The most common example of an affirmative defense is the statute of limitations, meaning the plaintiff had to bring a complaint within a certain amount of time (such as six years in some breach of contract cases). If the plaintiff filed their complaint outside of this window, you should allege as much as an affirmative defense. It is important to note that affirmative defenses are usually waived if they are not alleged in the answer. If you are unsure if an affirmative defense applies, it is always best to err on the side of caution and allege it anyway.

Counterclaims:

If the defendant has valid COUNTERCLAIMS, they should allege them after their affirmative defenses (they should also title their answer as "ANSWER AND COUNTERCLAIMS" in the caption). A counterclaim is simply a valid civil claim arising from the same set of circumstances. In breach of contract cases, for example, it is common for the defendant to allege that it was the plaintiff who, in fact, breached the contract. In this case, the defendant would make a breach of contract claim in their answer, in much the same way they would if they were the plaintiff making the allegations in a complaint. The defendant must allege all the elements of any claim they bring against the plaintiff as a counterclaim and allege the amount of damages they incurred. The plaintiff will then have to answer the counterclaim in the same way a defendant originally answered the complaint (but note that the identifiers of plaintiff/defendant remain the same). Appendix 1 includes a sample of an answer with counterclaims from the state of Oregon.

Filing and Serving the Answer

Once you have drafted your answer, you will need to file it at the county courthouse and pay the applicable filing fee. If you have limited financial means, you may be able to qualify for a fee waiver/deferral, but (as with plaintiffs) the standard for approval is quite high. If you think you may be approved, ask the clerk for a fee waiver application.

Next, you will have to serve a copy of the answer on the plaintiff. When filing a complaint, a plaintiff (or their attorney) are required to list an address where they can be served with legal documents in the case. This address should be on the last page of the complaint, beneath their signature, and/or on the first page of the complaint. After filing the answer, simply mail a copy to the plaintiff or their attorney along with a certificate of service.

Final Thoughts:

For the purposes of filing an answer, you only need to admit or deny the allegations in the complaint. You do not need to offer specific reasons for your denials. That said, you should keep in mind any potential defenses when denying the plaintiff's claims and think about how to introduce evidence later that would support them.

CHAPTER 4:
Pretrial Motion Practice

Motion Practice Generally:

Generally, a defendant should file an answer to a plaintiff's complaint. However, it is possible that they may try to file a motion first if they think the complaint has serious deficiencies. You should be aware of some of the potential motions a party may have to file and how to respond to them. The following sections contain a succinct review of the most common motions faced by *pro se* plaintiffs. It is generally not recommended that *pro se* litigants try to file any pretrial motions if they can help it, especially if the other side is represented by an attorney. Nevertheless, this chapter will provide useful information if you think filing a motion in your case is warranted or if you need to file a response to a motion.

If a defendant thinks a plaintiff's case has severe problems, they can attempt to get the case dismissed without the bother of going to trial or arbitration. This most often takes the form of a Motion to Dismiss and/or a Motion for Summary Judgment (discussed in more detail below).[3] When a motion is filed, the opposing party will have a certain amount of time to

---

[3] Note that motions for summary judgment are usually not filed until after an answer has been filed and the discovery process is complete, but they are discussed in this chapter as the process is generally similar to other pretrial motions.

file a RESPONSE. Then, the party who filed the initial motion will have a somewhat shorter time to file a REPLY to the response.

After a reply is filed, a date will be set for oral argument (although in some cases a judge may rule on the motions without hearing oral argument if they feel the issue is a simple one). At oral argument, both parties will have the opportunity to present their case to the judge, emphasizing and/or elaborating on their most important points. The judge will then either make a decision on the spot or issue an order at a later date if they want to review the issues more thoroughly.

Early Motions:

Some motions are filed by defendants at the outset of litigation instead of filing an answer. They are filed because the defendant thinks there is some sort of deficiency in the complaint that does not rely on the alleged facts. In other words, even if all the facts alleged by the plaintiff are 100% true, their claim would still fail for legal reasons. If the motion is granted, the plaintiff's case will either be dismissed (with or without prejudice depending on the nature of the motion) or the plaintiff will be forced to amend their complaint so that it corrects the deficiencies alleged in the motion. The most common types of early motions are:

Motion to Make More Definite and Certain:

This type of motion is filed when the plaintiff has done such a poor job of writing their complaint that the defendant cannot determine what, exactly, is being alleged. It is commonly filed against *pro se* plaintiffs who did not take the time to make sure their complaint was written correctly. If you follow the advice in this guide, keeping your complaint concise and only alleging material facts that are relevant to the elements of your claim, you should not have to worry about this type of motion.

How to Respond:

Your best response to this type of motion is that even if your complaint is not written perfectly, the defendant is not prejudiced by its form in any way and they can still mount a proper defense to your claims. That said, you should take the defendant's concerns seriously and if you can make your complaint clearer while still alleging all the elements of your claim, you should be agreeable to doing so. Do not assume that just because a motion is filed the defendant is trying to destroy your case. Fortunately, even if such a motion is granted, you will almost certainly be given leave to amend your complaint so your case can still go forward.

Motion to Strike:

This type of motion is filed to eliminate frivolous and irrelevant facts from a plaintiff's complaint. Again, if you follow the advice in this guide, you should not have to worry about a motion to strike being filed. However, defense attorneys are sometimes inclined to file such a motion to rattle *pro se* plaintiffs.

How to Respond:

Do not be intimidated. If the facts you have alleged are relevant to a claim or potential defense, state as much in your response. In addition, you should also add that even if some of the allegations in the complaint are not strictly relevant, the defendant will not be prejudiced in any way by leaving them in. You can state that it is your belief that the motion serves no purpose other than to harass and intimidate the plaintiff (judges do not expect a complaint written by a *pro se* plaintiff to be perfect and they may be irritated by the defendant's attorney if the judge thinks they are trying to harass you).

Motion to Dismiss:

A motion to dismiss usually alleges that the complaint, as written, does not allege the proper elements of a claim for relief. Depending on the nature of the motion, the defendant may seek to dismiss the complaint with or without prejudice. If the judge thinks that the deficiencies in a complaint can be amended, they will either dismiss the complaint without prejudice or give you leave to amend the complaint within a certain amount of time.[4] For example, if the statute of limitations on your claim is two years, and you allege in your complaint that the relevant events took place over two years ago, the judge will most likely dismiss the case with prejudice as no amendment could possibly cure the deficiency in the complaint.[5]

Often, a motion to dismiss is filed because a plaintiff has not alleged the proper elements of the claim in question. For example, if you file a breach of contract lawsuit, but you do not allege that consideration was given for the contract, a motion to dismiss would likely be granted (albeit with leave to amend) since you have not alleged facts sufficient to support the elements of your claim.

How to Respond:

Since the facts are not being disputed in a motion to dismiss, responding can be difficult. If you left out a material element of your

---

[4] If the judge rules against you, you should always ask for leave to amend rather than dismissal without prejudice. A dismissal without prejudice would mean the whole case would have to start over; whereas leave to amend will keep the proceedings moving forward with the same case number and you will not have to pay a new filing fee.

[5] This assumes that you alleged the date of the events properly. If you simply made a mistake or a typo regarding when the relevant events occurred, the judge will allow you to amend the complaint.

claim, ask for leave to amend in your response (assuming the facts to support the element in question can be alleged in good faith). Better yet, you and the opposing party should be able to agree on your amendment without the bother of filing a motion and response. Issues involving statutes of limitation and jurisdiction are usually more cut and dry and defending against them will be difficult. It is very important for a plaintiff to review these issues before filing the complaint to ensure you will not face dismissal early in the proceedings.

If a defendant files a motion to dismiss with prejudice and it is granted, the plaintiff should be able to appeal that decision to the state's appellate court. You should definitely speak to an attorney if you think an appeal is possible. If the motion is granted, but the claim is dismissed without prejudice and/or with leave to amend, there usually is not a right to appeal since your claims can still move forward. Appeals are generally only allowed when there has been a final decision that would end your case.

Motions for Summary Judgment

Unlike early trial motions, motions for summary judgment (if they are filed at all) are typically filed after discovery is complete. These motions take into consideration all of the available evidence. In a motion for summary judgment, the filing party makes the argument that the material facts of the case are undisputed and so one-sided that no reasonable judge or jury could possibly rule in favor of the opposing party.

For example, in a breach of contract case let us suppose the following:

- Plaintiff alleges that he painted Defendant's house in exchange for $10,000;

- Plaintiff alleges that this was done pursuant to an oral agreement;

- Defendant never paid Plaintiff.

If, during a deposition, Defendant admitted that all these allegations are true, then Plaintiff would have a strong case to file a summary judgment motion as there are no material facts in dispute (a transcript of the deposition should be attached as an exhibit). No judge or jury could reasonably find for defendant given his own testimony wherein he admits he breached the contract. If defendant instead admitted that he only paid plaintiff $5,000 because that was the agreed upon price, then summary judgment would be improper because there is a genuine issue of material fact as to whether the agreed upon price was $5,000 or $10,000. A jury (or judge/arbitrator in a bench trial/arbitration) would need to review the evidence at trial or arbitration and decide whose version of the facts is more credible. While most summary judgment issues may be a bit more complicated than this, the general idea is always the same.

When a summary judgment motion is filed, the opposing party (as with all motions) will have a set period of time to file a response. The party who initially filed the motions will then get to file a reply. During the summary judgment process, relying on allegations in a complaint to support your motion or response is not good enough. You must rely on actual evidence submitted as exhibits to your motion or response. This most often takes the form of deposition transcripts and written documentation obtained during discovery.

If you are a *pro se* litigant, it is probably a good idea not to attempt filing a motion for summary judgment. The facts of most cases are almost always in dispute and, if you are proceeding to a bench trial or arbitration, the judge/arbitrator will be the person weighing the evidence anyway, so there isn't much of a difference if the judge/arbitrator reviews it in a summary judgment motion or at trial/arbitration.[6] That said, if you believe filing a summary judgment motion is absolutely necessary, follow these guidelines:

- In some jurisdictions, courts prefer the motion and the memorandum supporting the motion to be in two separate documents. In other words, you would file a motion for summary judgment, wherein you simply ask the court to grant your motion and dismiss the opposing party's claims or defenses. You would also file a memorandum in support of your motion, wherein you lay out all your legal arguments and factual assertions. That said, it is common in many jurisdictions to have the memorandum and motion in the same document and the guidelines below are written with that presumption.

- If you would like the opportunity for oral argument, you should state as much in the caption of your case or the first paragraph of your motion.

- Next is the actual 'Motion' section, which is a simple sentence explaining what you are asking the court to do (such as dismiss Plaintiff's claims).

- Next is a simple case summary. Although the judge deciding the motion will have read the complaint and answer, a short summary of the issues at hand will help them follow your line of reasoning.

- Next is the 'Undisputed Material Facts' section. This should be a recitation of all the relevant facts that are proven in the record.

---

[6] Whereas, in a jury trial, you may want to avoid going in front of a jury, even if you feel the facts are indisputable, as juries can often be unpredictable even in the best of circumstances.

Each fact must have a citation to an exhibit or to an admission in the opposing party's pleadings or response to a request for admissions. Other than pleadings that have been filed in the proceedings, each document that you cite must be included as an exhibit with the motion for summary judgment. The judge will only look at the facts included with the motion. They will not assume any fact is true if you do not have some sort of documentation supporting it. Nor will they assume any fact is true if there is any reasonable interpretation (supported by evidence) that contradicts your own.

- The next section is the 'Argument'. Here, you will need to list each element of your claim and then refer to the facts that support it by citing to the particular page of each exhibit.

- Finally, there is the 'Conclusion', which can be a simple, one-sentence statement that asks the court to grant your motion.

In addition to the actual motion for summary judgment and the exhibits, you must also include a declaration where you authenticate all your exhibits and make any other factual statements (based on personal knowledge) that are relevant.[7] In other words, you tell the court why each exhibit should be trusted and what factual knowledge you have that supports your arguments.

After the opposing party files their response, you can file a reply to address any issues they brought up in the response. You cannot use the reply to bring up additional arguments that were not in your original motion unless they are directly addressing a point brought up in the response.

---

[7] Declarations based on personal knowledge from other people should be included as separate exhibits.

Regardless of whether or not you are a plaintiff or defendant, you may be forced to respond to a summary judgment motion. Your response should be formatted in a manner similar to the opposing side's motion:

- In the 'Undisputed Material Facts' section, state whether or not you agree with the opposing party's material facts. If you disagree with their characterization, be sure to say so in your response. You should also add any additional facts you feel are relevant. Just remember that you must have evidence you can cite to in order to support any fact you allege in your response or any fact you contradict in the opposing party's motion.

- You will also have to file a declaration authenticating your exhibits if you have added any exhibits to your response.

- Remember that when responding to a motion for summary judgment, you only need to show that there are material issues of fact that are in dispute. Summary judgment is proper only when there is a single reasonable interpretation of the facts. Otherwise, a judge or jury needs to weigh all the evidence at trial.

A sample summary judgment response form the State of Oregon is included in Appendix 1.

If a party's motion for summary judgment is granted, the opposing party can file an appeal. If a motion for summary judgment is denied, appeal is generally not possible because it is not a final adjudication, as the party who filed the motion can still make their case in front of a judge or jury.

The information above is a very brief overview of pretrial motion practice. Again, if you are a *pro se* litigant, it is probably best to avoid this area of law, as motions often hinge on a thorough interpretation of case law and existing legal precedent. However, if you can't avoid filing a motion or response, this chapter will give you the knowledge you need to make your case. If no early motions are filed or they have been filed and resolved, the next step of the civil process is to obtain evidence to support your case.

CHAPTER 5:
The Discovery Process

After the complaint and answer have both been filed and served, the next step in the litigation process is called 'Discovery'. Discovery is the process in which a party to a lawsuit has the right to obtain evidence directly from the other party. Litigants are obligated to engage in the discovery process in good faith and the penalties for failing to do so can be severe. In other words, if you are in possession of any evidence that may harm your case, you are legally obligated to disclose it!

The vast majority of discovery consists of REQUESTS FOR PRODUCTION OF DOCUMENTS (RFPs), REQUESTS FOR ADMISSIONS (RFAs), and DEPOSITIONS. This guide will show you how to engage in all three[8].

Note: This chapter pertains to obtaining evidence from parties to the lawsuit, which is a somewhat different process than obtaining evidence from other people not actively involved in the lawsuit. For advice on how to obtain evidence from non-parties, see Chapter 6.

---

[8] Note that INTERROGATORIES are also common in some jurisdictions, which (as stated in the glossary) are simply a written list of questions that is served upon the opposing party in a similar manner as a request for admissions.

Requests for Production

The RFP is a vital tool in any civil proceeding. As with many other aspects of the legal field, the concept behind all the legalese is quite simple. The RFP is simply a demand for documents that are relevant to the case. For example, in a civil claim for unpaid wages, the plaintiff/employee will want records of his/her timesheets and the defendant/employer is legally obligated to provide them (assuming they exist). It is important to note that documents that are required to be produced during discovery are *not* necessarily admissible at trial or arbitration. Documents that do not comply with your state's rules of evidence can still be objected to if/when the opposing party tries to admit them into evidence, but they must still be produced during discovery if they are at all relevant to a claim or defense.

Writing the RFP:

When drafting the requests, try to keep things as simple and narrow as possible. Do not ask for more information than you need as this will lead to objections from the opposing party (more on that below). For example, if you have filed a complaint for unpaid wages you feel you were owed throughout 2017, you probably do not need copies of your timesheets from 2015.

If you are the plaintiff, review the elements of your claim. What documents would help you prove each element? Those are what you should ask for. Next, review the defendant's answer. What documentation might they possess that would help prove any of their denials and defenses? For example, if the defendant in an unpaid wages lawsuit states that the plaintiff was indeed paid on time, you should definitely have a request that asks for copies of the specific paychecks the defendant is claiming were issued to the plaintiff (as well as any other records evidencing a payment was made).

Samples of a request for production and request for admission are included in Appendix 1.

Responding to an RFP:

If you are involved in a civil lawsuit of any kind (other than most small claims actions), you will most likely receive an RFP yourself. Most RFPs sent by attorneys are much broader than they need to be, often asking for documents that are outside the scope of litigation, such as medical records for any/all injuries (even if you are only claiming injury to a specific body part) and/or a party's entire social media history. When faced with any request you feel is irrelevant to the case, you have three options:

1. Object to the request consistent with your state's rules of civil procedure;

2. Comply with the request either partially or in full (if you are only partially complying, make sure you also list your objection as to why you are not complying in full).

3. Inform the other party that you do not have any of the documents they asked for.

Objections:

Generally speaking, there are three main objections to discovery requests:

1. The request is unlikely to lead to production of any admissible evidence. Note that discovery is generally broad, so this

objection should be used sparingly. If it is even potentially relevant to a claim or defense, the request should be honored.

2. The request is unduly burdensome. This means that complying with the request would require so much time and effort that the party should not be required to produce everything asked for. This objection often overlaps with the unlikely to lead to admissible evidence objection, as the broader a request gets, the less likely it is that anything relevant to a claim or defense will be produced.

3. The request asks for documents that would be privileged, such as communications between a party and their attorney. This is really a subset of the first objection, as if the requested documents are privileged, there is no way they can lead to admissible evidence (because the rules of evidence specifically exclude these types of communications).

When deciding whether or not to object to a request, do not object simply because you may have good cause to do so. If it is easy to produce the documents, you are better off doing so rather than arguing about whether or not it is relevant. If the documents requested are not relevant, then there should be no harm in producing them (unless doing so is unduly burdensome). Conversely, if they are relevant, you most likely will not have a valid reason to object in the first place.

Partial vs. Full Responses to a Request:

If you feel that the opposing party's request is reasonable and you have no issues responding to the request, then compile the documents, stamp them (see below) and send them to the opposing party.

If you feel that the opposing party's request is unreasonable, you may object. However, often a party's request will be partially reasonable and partially unreasonable. For example, if a request asks for three years of payroll records, but the alleged unpaid wages are only related to one year, the responding party should object in part, but still produce the documents they feel are relevant.

Even if you are objecting to some of the specific requests, it is vital to add the objection and serve your response on the opposing party within the timeline set by your jurisdiction. Otherwise, the opposing party may try and claim that you have waived any and all objections to that request.[9] If you need an extension of time to respond, politely ask the opposing party for as much time as you need. Make sure you do so via email if at all possible so there will be a record of your request.

When the Documents Don't Exist:

If you do not possess any of the documents requested, simply state: "No such documents are within [Plaintiff/Defendant]'s custody or control." However, note the 'custody or control' language. If you know where the documents are and they are not easily obtainable by the opposing party, but are easily obtainable by you, you must still produce them. For example, if a request asks for documents that you do not possess, but you know a friend or family member has them (and they would willingly give you a copy), such documents would be considered within your control and you must produce them. Likewise, if a request

---

[9] If, in a motion to compel, a party claims you have waived your objections by not responding in time, you should inform the judge in your response that you are formally requesting additional time to file your objections (even if your request is made after the original deadline). Most judges will grant such a request to pro se litigants, but try to avoid this issue in the first place by timely filing your responses and objections.

asks for bank records that you do not actually have, but can easily obtain from your bank, you must produce them.

The Final Response:

Once you have gathered all the relevant documents and you are ready to respond, follow these simple steps:

1. Ask for an MS Word copy of the opposing party's RFP. Any reasonable person should provide this as it will make reading your responses that much easier for them (likewise you should provide one, if asked). In fact, it is even a legal requirement in some jurisdictions. This allows you to enter your responses below each request without having to retype everything.[10]

2. Next, enter your responses and objections. All responsive documents need to be labeled with an identifier and page number that runs continuously through all requests and the actual documents must have a corresponding stamp. Using the party's last name is most common. For example, if Request 1 is 13 pages long, you would state: "[Plaintiff/Defendant] produces documents stamped as 'Smith 1-13'." Then, for Request 2, if there are 10 pages of documents, you would state: "[Plaintiff/Defendant] produces documents stamped as 'Smith 14-23'."

3. The best way to stamp your documents is to scan each response as a separate PDF file and use a computer program to add the appropriate stamp. We recommend using PDFill (available here: http://www.pdfill.com/), which is a free program that

---

[10] If they do not provide you a copy of their RFP do not feel obligated to retype the full text of their specific requests. Simply summarize each request in 2-3 words instead.

contains many other useful features (such as splitting and reordering pages). If you do not have the ability to electronically stamp your documents, you should label each page by hand (although there will probably be no repercussions if you fail to label them at all).

4. Most opposing parties will want documents in PDF file format on a CD-ROM, but be sure to review the instructions in the request for production you received. When you are a *pro se* litigant, most attorneys will be happy just to receive the documents (even if they aren't stamped), but professional courtesy demands that you make an effort to comply with their instructions and produce the documents in the format they have asked for. If the specific instructions are difficult for you to comply with, simply ask the other party (or their attorney) if they have any problems with your proposed method of production.

5. When everything is ready to go, mail the documents to the opposing party. The actual response to the RFP should be on paper and all the actual documents should be on the CD (but again, check the specific instructions). If you only have a few pages of documents to produce, you can just mail hard copies to the opposing party.

Problems with the Other Party's Response:

When you receive a response to the RFP you have sent to the opposing party, it will most likely contain similar objections to the ones discussed above. If they have failed to produce documents that you believe are relevant, the first step is to call the opposing party's attorney (or call them directly if they are not represented) and try to seek clarification as to why they think they are not obligated to produce the documents in question. Of course, you should also be prepared to state how they are directly relevant to any claim or defense at issue. Such conferral may be required before any further action is taken, depending on the rules of your state.

If you can't come to an agreement, you will have to get the court involved and file a MOTION TO COMPEL PRODUCTION OF DOCUMENTS. Your motion should be simple and direct. Simply explain the relevant elements of the claim or defense in question and how the documents requested would help prove or disprove such a claim. Once the reply (if any) is filed, the motion will be considered under advisement by the court and oral argument will be scheduled if it was requested by either party, at which point the judge will make their decision and give the opposing party a certain number of days to produce the documents if they have ruled in your favor. If the motion is denied, you will have to proceed without the requested documents. A sample RFP and motion to compel from the State of Oregon are included in Appendix 1.

Requests for Admissions

A Request for Admissions is precisely what it sounds like. It is a request that asks an opposing party to admit or deny a specific fact. Attorneys will often use RFA's to distill the factual issues. For example, in an unpaid wages case, an attorney may issue a request for admission stating, "Does Plaintiff admit or deny that their hourly wage at the time they were terminated by Defendant was $20.50 per hour." If Plaintiff were to admit this fact, that is one less piece of evidence that the parties will have to introduce later because the actual amount of Plaintiff's pay is not in dispute (thus saving the parties from introducing pay stubs or employment agreements that evidence Plaintiff's rate of pay).

Sending RFAs is not recommended for *pro se* litigants, especially if the opposing party is represented by an attorney. You will have more than enough on your plate dealing with other aspects of the discovery process and the opposing party's attorney will likely make sure their client does not admit to anything that would harm their case. However, you may very well be required to respond to the opposing party's RFA. In that case, keep in mind the following:

- Do not admit to anything if there is a shred of doubt regarding the matter. Even if it is a seemingly innocuous issue. So long as you cannot admit the request with 100% certainty, simply state, "Plaintiff/Defendant does not have sufficient factual knowledge to admit or deny Request XX. Therefore, it is DENIED."

- That said, do not deny a request in bad faith, either. If you were fired from your job on 1/31/2018, and you have a copy of the termination letter with that same date on it, you should probably admit that you were indeed fired on that date (assuming no contradictory evidence exists).

- Make sure you respond to the RFAs within the required timeline. If you fail to do so, the opposing party might try to get the court to treat all RFAs as admitted. If this happens, ask the judge for an extension of time to respond to the RFAs, just as you would for an RFP (see above).

- As with an RFP, you can request an MS Word copy of the RFA to make responding easier.

Depositions

Should I Schedule a Deposition?

The process for scheduling and conducting a deposition is not difficult. However, conducting depositions can be costly as you will have to hire a court reporter and you will need to order transcripts of the deposition if you plan on introducing any of the testimony as evidence at trial or in a motion. Given that this guide is intended to help people with limited financial means, depositions may be unrealistic for many people reading this guide. Furthermore, deposing third parties may not be necessary as you are free to talk about your case with them at any time. Assuming they are friendly and are willing/able to testify at trial, there is no need to formally depose them. If they will not be available to testify later you may be able to take their deposition and then use that testimony as evidence at trial, but you definitely need to check the relevant rules in your state regarding 'perpetuation of witness testimony'.

The only time you would need to depose a third party is if they are an uncooperative witness, in which case you will need to subpoena them to force them to appear, just as if you were subpoenaing them for trial (see 'Chapter 6 for more information on the subpoena process)[11]. You will also need to send the opposing party a notice of deposition and allow them to attend if they so desire. The actual deposition procedure is the same, regardless of who is being deposed. Rather than deposing third parties, however, you will most likely want to depose the opposing party (or employees of the opposing party) to gather more information about your case.

---

[11] If you are confident the person will show up for the deposition, a subpoena is not necessary.

Scheduling Depositions of Opposing Parties:

Although depositions can generally be held any time after an answer has been filed, it is standard procedure to issue and respond to RFPs first and then conduct a deposition, as the documentation produced often raises many questions that a party will want answered. The procedure for scheduling the deposition of a party to the litigation and a third-party witness is somewhat different, but the process of actually deposing them is the same. If you want to depose the opposing party or an employee of the opposing party, you probably do not need to worry about sending them a subpoena or witness appearance fee.[12]

Scheduling depositions usually begins by both parties informally discussing a proposed schedule of who they want to depose. Once a schedule is worked out, a NOTICE OF DEPOSITION should be sent to the opposing party or their attorney. Note that you will need office space to conduct the deposition. If you do not have an office and the opposing party is represented by an attorney, you should be able to use their office space. If not, you will have to find a location that is acceptable to both parties. Your local library, law library and/or courthouse may have space available. If you hire a court reporter from a larger company, they may have discounted or even free conference room space as well.

Hiring a Court Reporter:

You will also need to hire a court reporter who will record everything that is said at the deposition. A simple internet search will reveal court reporters working in your area. The cost to hire a court reporter is usually between $50-60 per hour. However, this does not include a

---

[12] Although if for some reason, the opposing party is not cooperating in the scheduling of depositions, you can seek a subpoena and compel them to appear.

transcript of the proceedings, which can often cost much more ($3-4 per page is common, with a two-hour deposition comprising approximately 80 pages). This means that the total cost for a 2-hour deposition would likely be around $450. Note that you may not need to order a copy of the transcript if you feel that the testimony of the party did not significantly help or harm your case and you are not planning on using it as an exhibit. Likewise, if you feel the party will not significantly change their story when they testify at trial, having a copy of the transcript may not be necessary. In either of those cases, you would only have to pay for the court reporter's time.

Conducting the Deposition:

On the day of the deposition, you should come prepared with a list of questions to ask the person being deposed (the deponent). When the deposition begins, the court reporter will administer the oath (wherein the deponent swears to tell the truth under penalty of perjury). You will then ask your questions. When deposing a witness, keep in mind the following:

- Do not interrupt or talk over the witness and remind them to try and refrain from doing the same thing.

- Keep your questions precise and tailored to the issues at hand. Remember, you only need to know information that proves or disproves any claim or defense. You don't need to know where the deponent went to grade school.

- Do not be intimidated if the deponent's attorney objects to your question (more on this below).

- Do not be afraid to ask follow up questions or ask for clarification.

- You can take a break anytime you want, but you must wait until the witness has answered the current question. If you want to step out or confer with the deponent's attorney, simply ask the court reporter, "Can we go off the record, please?" The court reporter will then stop recording everything and you are free to resume the deposition whenever everyone is ready.

When you are done asking your questions, the deposition is over (although sometimes opposing counsel will want to ask a few clarifying questions on the record). The court reporter will ask if you want to order a transcript. It is generally best to hold off until you are sure you need a copy. You can always contact the court reporter any time after the deposition to order a transcript. Just make sure you give them plenty of time to prepare the transcript if you have a trial or arbitration date approaching.

Submitting Evidence:

If you are deposing someone, you will most likely want to ask them about some of the documents you have received or produced in discovery. Therefore, you will need to have a list of exhibits ready to submit. You will need to bring three copies of each exhibit (one for the deponent/court reporter, one for the deponent's attorney, and one for yourself). If the deponent is not represented by an attorney, only two copies of each exhibit are necessary. Each exhibit should be marked and paginated (Exhibit 1, page 1, etc.).

When you are ready to have the deponent review an exhibit, simply tell them you would like them to review the following document labeled as "Exhibit X" and hand a copy to the court reporter (who will put their own label on it and then hand it to the deponent) and the deponent's attorney.

Deposition Objections:

If the deponent has an attorney, they may offer objections throughout the course of the deposition. Do not be too concerned. Most deposition objections relate to the form of a question. That is, if the question is confusing, it could lead to an answer that isn't clear. The opposing attorney may object to the form of the question and ask you to state it a different way. You should take their concerns seriously and if you think you can be clearer, you should try to restate your question. That said, do not be afraid to demand an answer from the deponent if you feel your question is perfectly clear and important to the matter at hand. The opposing attorney should then instruct their client to answer to the best of their ability.

In rare circumstances a deponent's attorney may instruct the deponent not to answer a question. This should only happen if you are asking for privileged information (such as details of a conversation they had with their attorney) or your questions are so far out of bounds and offensive that they amount to harassment. If you follow the advice in this guide, such scenarios should not occur. In the unlikely event that the deponent refuses to answer a question that is genuinely vital to the case at hand, you can file a motion to compel their answer in the same manner you would file a motion to compel production of documents.

If you follow the advice in this guide, you will be well on your way to compiling evidence to support your claims. Of course, there may very well be additional evidence that is not in possession of the defendant, which is the subject of Chapter 6.

CHAPTER 6:
How to Find and Prepare Evidence

As part of the discovery process, you will likely depose the opposing party and send them an RFP. In addition, you may want to obtain documents and testimony from people not directly involved in the lawsuit. This involves subpoenaing evidence and witnesses.

A plaintiff proves his or her case by submitting evidence that shows each element of their claim is present. Likewise, a defendant will attempt to show that plaintiff has not proven all the elements of their claim by also submitting evidence. The vast majority of evidence consists of witness testimony and written documentation. Most civil cases will involve both. Your state will have an Evidence Code that governs what is and is not considered admissible evidence. Follow the steps below to procure your evidence and prepare it for trial. Submitting evidence at trial and properly objecting to your opponent's evidence are both discussed in Chapter 9.

Procuring Witnesses and Exhibits

Procuring Witnesses:

Put simply, a witness is anyone who testifies under oath in a court proceeding. Generally speaking, a witness should have firsthand knowledge of the events they are testifying about (if they do not have firsthand knowledge, the opposing side will likely object to their testimony as hearsay – see Chapter 9). Below are three examples of situations that could (and often do) end up in civil court. Below the examples are a list of who could potentially be a valuable witness:

EXAMPLE 1:

- Plaintiff claims they were shopping in a supermarket when they slipped and fell in a puddle of water, injuring their back. This caused Plaintiff $3,000 in medical bills and they will seek an additional $3,000 for pain, suffering, and inconvenience. In this type of negligence case, Plaintiff would allege that Defendant (the store owner) has a duty to keep their store safe for customers and by failing to keep the floors dry and clean, Defendant failed in that duty, causing Plaintiff damages.

EXAMPLE 2:

- Plaintiff claims that the defendant owed them $5,000 because they had entered into an oral agreement in which Plaintiff agreed to paint the outside of Defendant's house in exchange for $10,000. Defendant paid Plaintiff $5000 up front, but then failed to pay the additional $5000 after Plaintiff finished painting the house.

EXAMPLE 3:

- Plaintiff claims that Defendant (who is Plaintiff's former roommate) stole his flat screen television and antique motorcycle when Defendant moved out. Plaintiff seeks damages of $6,000, representing $1,000 for the value of the television, $3,000 for the value of the motorcycle, and $2,000 in non-economic damages for loss of use of the property and/or pain/suffering/inconvenience. In the alternative, Plaintiff seeks return of the property in good condition and $2,000 in non-economic damages for loss of use of the property and/or pain/suffering/inconvenience.

Using the above examples, potential witnesses for each scenario would be:

EXAMPLE 1:

- Other shoppers that saw Plaintiff fall or saw the puddle on the floor would be ideal here. Of course, unless they are companions of Plaintiff, he or she may not know their names or how to contact them. In addition, any employee of the grocery store that may have seen the puddle or had a duty to clean it up could provide valuable testimony (see below for information on how to procure the identity of such witnesses and how to compel them to testify at the hearing).

EXAMPLE 2:

- In this example, Plaintiff would want anyone who knew of the existence of the agreement to testify. Did someone help Plaintiff paint the house? Was this person aware of the terms of the agreement? If Plaintiff painted other houses, can someone testify as to what Plaintiff normally charged for similar jobs? Did Plaintiff complain to others about not getting paid the full amount around the time Defendant refused to pay?

EXAMPLE 3:

- Did Plaintiff have another roommate besides Defendant? Was someone with Plaintiff when he bought the TV or motorcycle? Has anyone seen Defendant in possession of the motorcycle and/or TV? Can anyone testify that Plaintiff used to own these items and how much he valued them?

Regardless of who ends up being a witness in your case, make sure that any witness you have testify is only testifying regarding a crucial element of your claim and try to avoid having multiple witnesses that will testify about the exact same thing.

If the witness is a friend or relative and you can trust them to show up at trial or a deposition, then you should not have any trouble making sure they are available to testify. However, what if you need an unfriendly witness to offer testimony? In that case, you will need to have the court issue a subpoena on your behalf that orders them to appear at the time and date of the trial/deposition.

How to Subpoena a Witness:

As officers of the court, attorneys in most states are allowed to subpoena witnesses and compel them to appear in court. As a *pro se* litigant, you do not have such power. Instead, you will need to fill out a subpoena yourself and then have the court issue the subpoena for you (but you will still be the one in charge of making sure the witness is actually served with a copy of the subpoena).

Next, you will need to serve the subpoena on the witness. In some states, subpoenas can be served by the party in the case, which means you do not have to pay for the sheriff or a private process server to deliver the subpoena.

In any case, subpoenas for witnesses usually need to be served personally. You cannot use alternative methods of service. In addition, most states require that witnesses be compensated for their time and reimbursed for travel costs (usually in the form of a per mile rate). Check your state statutes and rules of civil procedure to find out your state's witness and mileage fees.

When you issue a subpoena, you should include a check for the appropriate amount. To determine the proper mileage, use any mapping web application (google maps, etc.) to determine the proper roundtrip distance from the witness's address. Then, multiply that amount by the mileage rate and add it to the witness fee. It is helpful to write up a simple calculation and attach it to the subpoena, but it is not necessary.

Once the witness has been properly served with a court-issued subpoena and given the proper compensation, they are legally obligated to appear and answer your questions under oath. If the date arrives and the witness has not shown up, you will have good cause to request a new date for the trial or deposition (alternatively, if you feel the witness' testimony is not crucial and you are eager to have your day in court, you could proceed without them). Simply inform the judge/arbitrator that a key witness has failed to appear pursuant to a validly issued subpoena (make sure you have a copy available to review) and the interests of justice require that a new date be set so the witness can be heard.

Procuring Exhibits:

In addition to having witnesses testify on your behalf, you will usually want to submit written (or audio/video) evidence that also supports your claim and reinforces the testimony of your witnesses. An exhibit can essentially be anything, but 99% of the time, it will be some sort of document. As witnesses are often biased and have imperfect memories, cold, hard documentary evidence can be vital to proving a claim.

How to Identify Potential Exhibits:

As with witnesses, a relevant exhibit is anything that helps prove or disprove a party's claim or defense. Exhibits that are repetitive are usually unnecessary. Similarly, exhibits should be as concise as possible. Using the examples from earlier in the chapter, here are some types of written evidence that would be useful to both parties:

EXAMPLE 1:

- Medical bills that show any out of pocket medical expenses.

- Any kind of accident report that was filled out by the grocery store.

- Any cleaning logs that are maintained by the grocery store.

- Any emails, text messages, or other documents wherein Plaintiff describes his/her injuries and the pain, suffering, and/or inconvenience they have caused.

EXAMPLE 2:

- Any invoices or receipts sent to Defendant by Plaintiff.

- Any similar invoices or receipts from prior similar jobs performed by Plaintiff for other people.

- Any emails, text messages, or other documents wherein Plaintiff describes the work done for Defendant and how much Plaintiff was supposed to get paid.

EXAMPLE 3:

- Any receipt that shows what Plaintiff paid for the TV or motorcycle.

- A website or advertisement that shows the value of the same model of TV and motorcycle that were allegedly stolen by Defendant.

- Any receipts for maintenance that show Plaintiff paid for the upkeep of the TV and motorcycle.

- Any emails or text messages that Plaintiff sent to Defendant wherein the TV or motorcycle were discussed.

Once you are aware of what types of exhibits would be helpful in proving your claim or defense, you will need to obtain them. As with witnesses, exhibits can be obtained by having the court issue a subpoena. A subpoena for documents is referred to as a 'Subpoena Duces Tecum' (Latin for 'you shall bring with you')[13]. It is issued by the court the same way as a subpoena for a witness is issued. However, a subpoena duces tecum generally does not need to be served personally. It can usually be served via mail (certified mail is recommended, so you will have proof that the subpoena was sent).

If you think you need a police report to help prove your claims, you can usually obtain these without a subpoena. You will need to contact the relevant police department and inquire about their particular procedures for releasing police reports. Make sure you do so well in advance of your trial, as the process can take several weeks.

Once the subpoena form is complete, you will need to go to the courthouse and present it to the clerk at the civil filing window. The clerk will make sure everything is in order and then sign it and stamp it

---

[13] Although a person does not normally bring the documents 'with them'. Rather, they are commanded to deliver the documents to a specific location (usually via mail to the party's address). The person's actual appearance is not required.

with the court's seal (as with other subpoenas, this process may vary by state). This gives the subpoena duces tecum the official authority of the court and anyone who disregards it can potentially be found in contempt. Before you mail the subpoena duces tecum, you usually need to send a copy to the opposing party (to put them on notice of the documents you are seeking) and then wait a certain number of days. After that you can send the subpoena duces tecum to the addressee. You will also have to send any applicable witness fee along with the subpoena, but you do not need to include any mileage payment.

Once the person or entity has been properly served with a court-issued subpoena duces tecum and received the required witness fee, they are legally obligated to turn over the documents in question or face potential contempt charges. If the time to produce the documents has passed without a response, you should contact them directly and inform them that you will be pursuing contempt charges if they do not respond.[14] If the hearing date is approaching and you still do not have the documents that were requested pursuant to a valid subpoena, you can ask the court to delay the proceedings and/or seek contempt charges against the person/entity failing to produce the documents.

A sample of a subpoena and subpoena duces tecum from the State of Oregon are included in Appendix 1.

Preparing Exhibits:

On the day of your trial/arbitration, you will need to bring four copies of all your exhibits. One copy is for you, one for the opposing party, one for witnesses to review, and one for the judge/arbitrator. All exhibits must be numbered in the bottom right of the document, with

---

[14] If the person who was served believes they have good legal cause to disregard the subpoena, they should file a motion to quash the subpoena; not simply ignore it.

plaintiffs usually starting with the number 1 (Exhibit 1, Exhibit 2, etc.) and defendants usually starting with number 101 (Exhibit 101, Exhibit 102, etc.).

In addition to the exhibits being marked, they must also have individual page numbers (with each individual exhibit starting over with 'page 1'). The easiest way to label exhibits is to have them scanned as a PDF file and then use an editing tool to add the label. Again, we recommend using PDFill, which is free and can be downloaded here: http://www.pdfill.com. If you are unable to use a PDF file editor and/or you only have a few short exhibits, you can label each one by hand. If you are submitting photographs as exhibits, you should group them by subject and label each group as a different exhibit, with each individual photo having its own page number.

If you have more than a few exhibits, you should put each set of exhibits in a binder, but the most important thing is to make sure they are clearly labeled and each page can be referenced and viewed easily. You should also include a witness and exhibit list at the front of each set of exhibits. Simply list your exhibits in roughly the order you intend to introduce them and give a brief description of each one. Do the same for your witnesses.

Now that your exhibits and witnesses are prepared, you are almost ready for the trial or arbitration! Chapter 7 discusses the arbitration process generally, Chapter 8 discusses jury trials, and Chapter 9 discusses what to expect on the actual day of your trial or arbitration.[15]

---

[15] If your case is not subject to arbitration, you can skip Chapter 7.

CHAPTER 7:
Arbitration

In an effort to reduce the burden on state courts and resolve disputes faster, many states have instituted mandatory arbitration programs for many civil cases. Arbitration is a process wherein legal disputes are resolved outside of the court system. A neutral, mutually agreed upon arbitrator will act as a judge and jury, conduct a hearing, and make an ultimate decision in favor of one party. Courts in most states maintain a list of approved arbitrators. They must be a licensed attorney and will likely have several years of experience (indeed, many of them are former or part-time judges).

In addition to mandatory arbitration, many states allow the parties to mutually agree to binding arbitration instead of having their case heard in court. Also, many contracts have mandatory arbitration provisions that will need to be followed if you are suing for a breach of that contract.

Arbitration is meant to be a more efficient and less formal means of resolving legal disputes. As such, arbitration proceedings are held in a conference room (usually at the arbitrator's office), the rules of evidence are not strictly enforced, and a final hearing is always held much sooner than a trial would be scheduled. That said, you should still generally treat every arbitration hearing as you would an actual trial. You should label your exhibits in the same manner, examine witnesses in the same manner, and treat the arbitrator with the same respect you would treat a judge, even if you are sitting in a conference room instead of a courtroom.

Arbitration has many advantages and disadvantages:

- Advantage: It is a much quicker process than a regular trial. Arbitrations can often be completed within 3-4 months of filing a complaint, whereas waiting for an available judge for a jury or bench trial can often take a year or more.

- Disadvantage: It can often cost more than a jury trial. Generally, both parties must make a deposit to the court to pay the arbitrator for their time. The amount of the deposit varies by state, but it is not uncommon for arbitrators to charge $150-$200 per hour. The parties will be obligated to pay that amount, split equally. If, after all motions are filed and the arbitration is held and the arbitrator's billable time exceeds the initial deposit, both parties will likely need to make up the difference. What's more, the losing party is almost always ordered to pay the other party's costs and disbursements, which includes the full cost of the arbitrator.

- Advantage/Disadvantage: Arbitration proceedings are not bound by strict rules of evidence. In other words, the type of evidence submitted is held to less stringent requirements. For example, the arbitrator will often consider hearsay evidence and/or will accept the validity of documents without rigorous authentication. This can be good and bad, depending on the nature of the evidence available to you and the opposing party.

- Advantage/Disadvantage: Arbitration is not always binding. This means that if the arbitrator rules against you, you can appeal the decision and have your case proceed to a regular trial. The results of the arbitration will generally not be admissible so you will be starting with a clean slate. Conversely, even if you win at arbitration, the opposing party may likewise appeal the decision. On the plus side, if you lose, this does allow you a second chance to plead your case and it is not uncommon for arbitration decisions to be reversed at trial or for a settlement to be reached before the trial begins.

Overall, arbitration is usually worthwhile and should be participated in with enthusiasm. An arbitrator will be much more sympathetic to a *pro se* litigant than a jury and the less formal nature of an arbitration will serve you well. The cost can be a downside, but if you have a relatively simple claim, you should not require too much of the arbitrator's time.

CHAPTER 8:
Jury Trials

If you are a pro se litigant, it is ALWAYS preferable to avoid a jury trial. Jurors will assume that a plaintiff or defendant who could not find an attorney to represent them must not have a very strong case. While this is definitely not true and an unfair assumption, it would be very difficult to convince most jurors otherwise (yet another good reason to participate in arbitration instead). Most jurors will have never seen an actual trial, let alone one in which a party is representing themselves. A judge, on the other hand, will have dealt with pro se litigants on a regular basis. They will understand that not everyone can afford an attorney and just because you may not be an expert in civil procedure, your case may still have merit.

Unfortunately, the opposing party in most lawsuits usually has the right to a jury trial, so you may find yourself in front of a jury whether you like it or not. This chapter will provide a basic overview of the jury selection and instruction process, giving you the knowledge you need to ensure your jury trial proceeds smoothly.[16]

Jury Trial is usually the Default:

As mentioned above, it is never a good idea for a *pro se* litigant to participate in a jury trial. When you file your complaint or answer, most

---

[16] If your case is not going to be heard in front of a jury, you can skip this chapter.

courts will presume that a jury trial is desired. If both parties stipulate to a bench trial, they can inform the court and the case will be designated as a bench trial instead. Unfortunately, both sides usually have the right to a jury trial, so even if you prefer a bench trial, if the other side does not agree, the case may still be scheduled to go in front of a jury. Even if the opposing party has initially declined to agree to a bench trial, do not be afraid to ask them again when it gets closer to the trial date.

Jury Selection:

Every court and state will conduct jury selection a bit differently. However, the basics of jury selection are as follows:

1. On the first day of trial a pool of potential jurors will have already been selected. Depending on the court, some or all of the potential jurors will be brought into the courtroom and questioned about their qualifications.

2. Usually, the judge will ask some preliminary questions first, then the plaintiff will get to ask the jurors questions, followed by the defendant (see below for more information on how to examine jurors).

3. Next, the plaintiff may seek to exclude certain jurors if they feel the juror is biased in some way. Then, the defendant will get the same opportunity (this is done outside the presence of the jury). If good cause exists, an unlimited number of jurors can be excluded. After exclusion for cause is completed, if no cause exists, a party can usually exclude jurors with what are known as preemptory challenges.

    a. Exclusion for Cause: Most challenges based on good cause relate to basic qualifications of the juror, such as mental capacity, being related to a party, or not being a resident of the county. Ideally, the judge will ask the jurors these basic questions and exclude them without you having to worry about it.

The main type of exclusion for cause that you will need to be concerned about is exclusion due to bias. If, during your examination, you feel that a juror is genuinely biased based on his answers to your questions, do not be afraid to seek their exclusion for cause. The opposing party may object and it will be up to the judge to decide whether or not to grant the exclusion, but there is no downside. If the judge denies your request, you should still be able to use a preemptory challenge to exclude the juror.

b. Preemptory Challenges: If good cause does not exist to get a juror excluded for cause, but you still feel that they would not be sympathetic to your case, you can use a preemptory challenge to get a juror excluded. The number of preemptory challenges allowed will vary by state, but is usually two and three for each side. Preemptory challenges are made in an alternating manner until both sides have used up all their challenges (or no longer wish to exercise any remaining challenges).

No reason needs to be given for a preemptory challenge, but you cannot exclude a juror based on their race, ethnicity or sex. If the other side feels your preemptory challenge is based on one of these factors, they can object and you will have to offer a non-discriminatory reason for why you want that juror excluded (so do not be afraid to exclude someone who is the same race as the opposing party, so long as you can point to another legitimate reason for the exclusion).

4. Once the preemptory challenges are completed, the final jury will have been chosen (along with a couple of alternate jurors). The trial will then begin.

Juror Examination:

Examining jurors (known officially as *voir dire*[17]) can seem intimidating, but do not be too concerned. You have free reign to ask jurors any questions you feel may be relevant to whether or not they can hear the case in an impartial manner. For example, if you are suing a tow truck company for negligence, you definitely want to know if any potential juror (or member of their family) owns/works for a towing company. If you are suing your manager for discrimination, you want to know if any potential juror has ever been involved in a discrimination lawsuit or has a managerial job similar to the defendant's.

It is best to start with general questions (most likely asked in front of all the potential jurors, but check with your local court). For example, a good question to start with is, "Has anyone ever been a plaintiff or defendant in a civil lawsuit?" A number of potential jurors will likely raise their hand and you will then be able to follow up with each and every one of them. What was the nature of the lawsuit? What was the outcome? If you are suing your employer/manager for discrimination and a potential juror has also sued their employer for discrimination, you will likely want this person on the jury (although they will probably be excluded by the defendant with a preemptory challenge).

There are two websites that offer a very good guide to what jury selection is like and what kinds of questions are usually asked. The first is from the University of Missouri School of Law and can be found here: http://libraryguides.missouri.edu/c.php?g=28615&p=176509. It contains a

---

[17] Latin for 'to speak the truth'.

fictional transcript of jury selection as well as two actual transcripts. The second is a list of questions published by the State of New Jersey and can be found here: https://www.judiciary.state.nj.us/attorneys/assets/attyresources/jurorselectionquestions.pdf. It is intended as a guide for judges, but still contains several good examples of the types of questions that are typically asked during the jury selection process. Use these guides to formulate your own list of questions based on the facts of your individual case.

Jury Instructions:

Besides jury selection, the other major difference between a jury and a bench trial is that you are expected to formulate your own jury instructions (in most states). A jury requires detailed instructions on how to approach each and every aspect of your case. The court normally expects both parties to submit proposed jury instructions (usually before trial), but if both the litigants are *pro se*, the court will most likely use some form of model jury instructions (such as those published by the state bar). If instructions are submitted, the judge will review them and hear any objections from both sides before coming up with a final set of instructions that will be submitted to the jury (the exact process may differ slightly in each court). Your state's rules of civil procedure and/or trial court rules will govern the process for creating and submitting jury instructions, but you are probably better off not trying to submit your own instructions. However, you must be prepared to object to any proposed instructions provided by the opposing party if you think they are written in a biased, non-objective way.

That said, it will not hurt to be familiar with some of the more common instructions in your state. Most states will have some form of model jury instructions, which should be available for review and copying at your local law library.

Similar to jury instructions, a verdict form will also need to be submitted to the jury. The jury will use this form to write out the actual verdict. If a proposed verdict form is not submitted by a party, the court should be able to provide one.

Again, try to avoid a jury trial if at all possible. If it is unavoidable, the information in this chapter will serve you well. Once the jury is seated, the actual trial procedure will not be materially different than an arbitration or bench trial. You will still introduce evidence and examine witnesses in the same way. Chapter 9 discusses how to do so and what to expect on the day of the trial.

CHAPTER 9:
At the Hearing

This chapter goes over the basic steps involved in any evidentiary hearing in, whether it is a bench trial, arbitration, or jury trial. Do not be intimidated by the fact that you will be in a courtroom in front of a judge or presenting your case before an arbitrator[18]. With this guide you will be well prepared to prove your case!

Settlement Conferences:

Many courthouses require parties to attend a settlement conference before trial (if you are subject to mandatory arbitration you will probably not be required to attend a settlement conference). When a settlement conference is not required, one can usually still be requested by either party via motion and the other party will be required to participate in the settlement conference in good faith if the judge orders a conference. The settlement conference will usually take place at the county courthouse where a judge will act as a mediator and try to broker a settlement.

Regardless of whether or not you have an attorney, settlement conferences can be quite valuable. You will get an unbiased opinion from a judge with several years of experience on the merits of your case.

---

[18] For ease of use, the rest of this chapter will refer to being in front of a judge, but the information equally applies to being in front of an arbitrator (unless otherwise noted).

You should check your county courthouse's local rules for details on their settlement conference procedures, but most settlement judges will prefer that you submit a memo outlining the basic facts and the pros/cons of your case. Do *not* share this memo with the opposing party. It is for the judge only and it gives you a chance to be upfront about the deficiencies in your case, without letting the other side know your weaknesses. Judges expect the parties to be forthright in their settlement memos and they will be skeptical if you do not give an objective analysis of the potential weaknesses in your case.

If a settlement is reached at the conference, the judge will likely want to enter the basic terms on the record in order to make sure that one side doesn't renege on the terms later. If both sides are unrepresented, the judge will probably even draft a judgment and file it in the record at the conference. If one side is represented, their attorney will probably be tasked with preparing the judgment. If no settlement is reached, the case will proceed to trial.

At the Hearing:

A day or two before the hearing, you will want to submit a trial memorandum to the judge, wherein you describe how your case will proceed at trial and how you will go about proving your claims. You do not need to list individual exhibits or name individual witnesses, but you should cite the relevant elements of your claims and state how you intend to go about proving each one. Make sure you properly serve the opposing party at the same time you send the memo to the judge.

On the day of your hearing you should be prepared to present your case before the judge. You are, in all respects, acting as your own attorney and you should conduct yourself just as an attorney would to the extent possible. Here are some general guidelines:

- Get to court/arbitration early. Parking may be inconvenient, you will likely have to go through security (at a courthouse), and it may take time to find out which courtroom you are in. Make sure you give yourself time for all of these issues.

- Be respectful to the judge and the opposing party.

- Dress professionally. It is always surprising how many people show up to court in casual clothes. Although there is no dress code required for parties or witnesses, taking the time to dress professionally shows the judge that you are taking everything seriously and lends an air of respectability to your claims.

- DO NOT argue with the opposing party or speak out of turn in front of the judge. Both sides will have a chance to present their arguments, cross examine witnesses, and make a closing statement. There is no need to interrupt the other party when it is their turn to speak.

- Do not talk over the judge, the opposing party, or any witnesses.

- If you do not understand something the judge has said or how to proceed, simply ASK! A judge will not give you legal advice, but they will inform you if you need help with procedural questions.

- When addressing the judge, it is always proper to stand up first (do not stand when addressing an arbitrator). It is not necessary to stand when examining witnesses, but you may do so if you prefer. DO NOT roam around the courtroom like you may have seen on TV!

Steps at the Hearing:

In all civil cases, the hearing or trial will typically proceed as follows:

1. The judge will call your case by name and case number. When they do, you may approach the counsel table from the gallery. It is also possible that the judge will first want to have a meeting with both parties and/or their attorneys in the judge's chambers to discuss the general nature of the case.

2. Once the judge is sure everyone is ready and there are no procedural issues to deal with, they may ask the parties to make an opening statement (but some judges will want to proceed right to calling witnesses if it is a bench trial and you have submitted a trial memo). If you want to make an opening statement, but the judge seems to skip over this step, you can always ask to make one. Just keep it brief and summarize why you are entitled to relief.

3. At this point, the judge may want both parties to submit all their exhibits and offer any relevant objections (they may also do this in the pretrial meeting). If you feel you have good cause to object to any evidence being entered into the record inform the judge of the specific exhibit you are objecting to and why (see below for the most common objections you will deal with). Do not be afraid to object! The worst that will happen is that the judge will overrule your objection and the evidence will be received (which is what will definitely happen if you do not object). Alternatively, a judge will admit all stipulated exhibits and require that any

contested exhibits be entered during examination, at which point parties can object to their admission into the record.

4. The judge will then tell the plaintiff to call their first witness. Say, "Thank you, Your Honor. I call XXXX." At this point, the plaintiff's witness should proceed to the witness stand and he/she will be sworn in by the court clerk. Once sworn in, ask your questions (see below for more information). During questioning, the judge may interject with their own questions.

5. If the judge did not admit some or all of your exhibits at the beginning of the trial, you will need to make sure that your exhibits are admitted at the time they come up during witness testimony (regardless of which party has called the witness). For example, if you are interviewing a witness and ask them to review Exhibit 2, have the witness describe the exhibit, then say, "Your honor, I would like to admit Exhibit 2 into the record." The judge will give the opposing party an opportunity to object and then make a decision on whether or not the exhibit is received. The fact that you have already handed your exhibits to the witness and the judge does not mean they are admitted, unless the judge has already clearly stated as much before trial!

6. After the plaintiff has finished asking their witness questions, the defendant will have an opportunity to cross-examine the witness and ask him/her any questions that are relevant to any claim or defense. When the defendant is done with his cross examination, the plaintiff will have a chance to ask any follow up questions (called 'redirect examination'), but they will likely be restricted to only asking about issues that were brought up in the defendant's cross-examination (although the judge may grant a party some leniency in this regard if they are representing

themselves). After both parties have asked all their questions, the plaintiff will call their next witness.

7. Once the plaintiff has called all of their witnesses and introduced all their exhibits, they will inform the judge that they rest their case. If they still have exhibits that were not admitted during examination and they still want the judge to consider them, they will state that they have additional exhibits they would like to enter into the record.

8. At this point, the defendant will have the chance to call witnesses and introduce exhibits. The plaintiff will have the chance to cross examine each witness and object as appropriate.

9. After the defendant has called all of their witnesses and rested their case, the plaintiff will then have the chance to call rebuttal witnesses who can contradict the statements made by the defendant's witnesses. These can be new witnesses or witnesses who initially testified during the presentation of the plaintiff's case.

10. Once rebuttal testimony is complete, the judge will ask for a closing statement and/or if there is anything else either party would like to add. In your closing statement, inform the judge how you have proven each element of your claim, citing the specific testimony or exhibit that illustrates your point. The judge will likely make a ruling on the spot, but may issue a written opinion in a few days if they feel they need time to review the evidence. If you are participating in a jury trial, the jury will deliberate and inform the judge when they have reached a decision.

11. If the judge/jury rules in your favor, CONGRATULATIONS! You have successfully prosecuted/defended a civil case from start to finish! Refer to Chapter 10 for information on how to collect on your judgment.

12. If you are the plaintiff and the judge rules in the defendant's favor, you will have to pay their filing fee and any other court costs (such as arbitration fees). If the defendant filed a counterclaim against you, you will be ordered to pay on that claim as well. The judge (or the defendant's attorney) will prepare a judgment stating as much and your case will be over. It may be small consolation, but if you followed the steps in this guide, you can at least rest assured that you gave it your best shot and did everything you could to obtain relief.

13. How to appeal a final judgment is beyond the scope of this guide, but if you think you have good cause to appeal, you will need to do so within the time limit set by your state.

Examining Witnesses:

Whether you are the plaintiff or defendant, you will be expected to ask questions of each witness that are relevant to your claims or defenses. The first step is to establish why the witness is testifying. Who are they? How do they know the plaintiff/defendant? What knowledge do they have that proves an element of a claim or defense? As always, keep things simple and direct. Apply who, what, where, why, questions. Do not argue with the witness (but do not be afraid to ask for clarification if you feel their answer doesn't make sense or they are being evasive).

If you have exhibits that you want the witness to review, ask them to refer to your binder/pack and turn to the relevant exhibit. Usually, a witness will need to establish what a particular exhibit is before it can be discussed in more detail. Ask the witness if they recognize the document and if they can describe it for the court. At this point, if the particular exhibit has not been entered into the record during the pre-hearing phase, inform the judge that you seek to enter it now ("Your honor, I'd like to enter Exhibit 1 into the record"). The judge will then ask the opposing party if there are any objections. If there are no objections, or the objection is overruled, the exhibit will be received and entered into evidence (see below for more information regarding admissibility and objections). You can then ask more detailed questions about the nature of the exhibit and establish why it is important to your case. It is important to note that witness examination is not the time for you to offer your opinions on the nature of their testimony. If the witness admits to something that proves an element of your claim, do not interject and inform the court of this fact. Save such statements for your closing argument. You should only be asking questions and introducing exhibits to create a factual record.

Of course, in addition to examining witnesses, you will most likely want to testify yourself as well. With no attorney to ask you questions, you will simply offer your testimony directly to the court. Explain that you would like to call yourself as a witness (you will most likely be able to testify from the counsel table; rather than having to go up to the witness stand). After you are sworn in, you will then be able to offer your version of events in a clear and concise manner. If you want to review an exhibit, inform the court and the opposing party, tell the court why that particular exhibit is significant, and ask to enter it into the record (if it has not already been entered). Just remember that you are testifying; that is, you are stating facts on the record. Now is not the time to argue the merits of your case. Save all your opinions for your closing statement and simply stick to the facts.

That said, you can and should inform the court if you think the testimony of another witness is false or misleading, but you need to testify (based on personal knowledge) as to why that is the case. For example, when you are testifying, stating, "I think Witness XX is lying about being at the intersection at the time of the accident" would be inappropriate, but stating "I do not believe Witness XX is telling the truth because I was personally at the intersection at the time of the accident and I did not see him there." would be acceptable.

Objections:

If a party tries to submit evidence (via an exhibit or witness testimony) that is not allowed by your state's rules of evidence, the other party can object (but they are not required to do so). Objections to witness testimony should be offered after the question is asked, but before the witness answers (do not forget to stand up when objecting). However, sometimes it is impossible to object before the witness answers (as whether or not the statement is admissible will depend on what, exactly, is said). If an answer is inadmissible, you should still object and ask the judge to strike that specific witness testimony. (in a jury trial, the judge will inform the jury to disregard the testimony that was objected to). A full discussion of all the rules of evidence and their proper objections is beyond the scope of this guide. Fortunately, the vast majority of objections in any civil case fall into just two categories: Relevance and Hearsay. If you have a firm grasp of these two rules, you will be well prepared. Of course, you can (and should!) review your state's evidence code before your trial.

Relevance:

All states will have a rule of evidence regarding relevancy. For example, in Oregon, Rule 402 states: "All relevant evidence is admissible, except as otherwise provided by the Oregon Evidence Code, by the Constitutions of the United States and Oregon, or by Oregon statutory and decisional law. Evidence which is not relevant is not admissible."

Relevant evidence is often defined as evidence having any tendency to make the existence of any fact that is of consequence to the determination of the action more probable or less probable than it would be without the evidence.

Pretty straightforward, right? If evidence is relevant to any claim or defense, it is admissible. If it is not relevant, then it is not admissible and an objection should be made. Often, relevance objections come up when one party tries to discredit the other. Examples of irrelevant evidence might include:

- In a divorce trial, if the husband tried to introduce evidence of the wife being unfaithful, the wife should definitely object as such information is not relevant to how the assets of the marriage should be distributed or what parenting plan should be put in place (no fault divorce is the rule in each state).

- In a breach of contract case, evidence that the defendant breached a contract with a third party a year earlier would likely not be relevant to the present case (as prior bad acts are no indication that a party acted the same way in the present case as they did in the prior case).

- In a personal injury case involving damages for a broken arm, evidence that the plaintiff broke their leg a few years ago would not be relevant.

Although there are more detailed rules of evidence that may apply in some situations, think of the relevance objection as a catch-all objection and do not spend time trying to remember whether or not a more specific objection exists. So long as you can make the case that the evidence in question is not relevant to any claim or defense, offering an objection under the relevance rule is perfectly acceptable. If you are unsure of whether or not evidence is relevant, always err on the side of caution and object. The worst thing that will happen is that your objection will be overruled and the evidence will be entered into the record (which would happen anyway if you did not object).

Hearsay:

Hearsay is generally defined as: "A statement, other than one made by the declarant while testifying at the trial or hearing, offered in evidence to prove the truth of the matter asserted." A "statement" can be oral, written, or any type of nonverbal conduct. The "declarant" is simply the person who originally made the statement in the first place. In other words, a witness cannot testify that someone else told them something.[19] The person who actually made the statement needs to be present to testify. Examples of hearsay evidence include:

- In a custody hearing if the husband were to testify: "my wife's sister told me that my wife abuses the children when I am not around."

---

[19] Likewise, a document written by someone else cannot be admitted as an exhibit (unless an exception applies).

- In a breach of contract case, if the plaintiff were to testify: "Defendant's former employee told me that Defendant had no intention of honoring our agreement."

- In a personal injury case, if the plaintiff tried to submit a copy of a text message from a bystander that said they saw the defendant run a red light and hit the plaintiff's car.

Hearsay is generally excluded because it is difficult to corroborate such evidence. Anyone can say that anyone else told them a certain fact. Unless the person with personal, first-hand knowledge is present to testify under oath, hearsay evidence will usually be excluded. That said, if you are in arbitration, the arbitrator will often allow hearsay evidence so long as there is no serious doubt as to its authenticity. However, just because it is admitted does not mean the arbitrator will give the evidence any weight when making their decision.

Although hearsay evidence is generally inadmissible, there are several exceptions in each state. The most common hearsay exceptions relate to statements made by the party opponent (meaning a witness for the plaintiff can testify that the defendant told them something and vice versa) and business records, such as time sheets and paystubs. Do not trouble yourself with trying to learn all of the hearsay exceptions. When a party tries to admit hearsay evidence you should object and let the other party try to offer an exception. If hearsay evidence is admitted, regardless of whether or not you offered an objection, you should make a point of reminding the judge in your closing statement that the evidence should be given very little weight and the court should not consider it credible when making a decision.[20]

---

[20] On the other hand, if you are the one trying to admit hearsay evidence, you should argue the opposite: even if the evidence is hearsay, the person making the statement in court is sufficiently reliable and the judge should trust this person's sworn testimony when evaluating the merits of the case.

With a basic understanding of witness examination and the evidentiary objections of relevance and hearsay, you will be well equipped to professionally prosecute or defend your civil case at trial. Just remember to keep things focused on the elements of your specific claim or defense and be respectful of the judge and the opposing party. Win or lose, you should be proud that you took your case all the way through trial!

CHAPTER 10:
How to Collect on A Judgment

If you have prevailed in a civil lawsuit, you will likely have been awarded a certain amount of money as part of a judgment. Even if you are the defendant, you were likely awarded the cost of your filing fee and a small prevailing party fee. Unfortunately, winning in court is often only half the battle as many parties ordered to pay will refuse to do so. When this happens, the burden is on the person who is owed money to collect what is due.

If you have prevailed against a government agency or a large corporation, getting paid will likely not be a problem. But if you have a valid judgment against an individual, you may be required to undertake collection efforts. For *pro se* litigants, the two best courses of action are garnishing bank accounts and garnishing wages.

Relevant Definitions:

When trying to collect on a judgment, you should be familiar with the following terms:

- **Judgment Creditor:** A person who is owed money from a judgment debtor due to a court judgment (the prevailing party in a civil action).

- **Judgment Debtor:** A person who owes money to a judgment creditor due to a court judgment.

- **Writ of Garnishment:** A writ of garnishment is a court order that requires a third party (such as a bank or employer) to turn over property it holds or has control over that belong to the judgment debtor (such as bank account funds or wages).

- **Garnishee:** A third party who has been ordered to hand over any property of a judgment debtor it has in its custody or control.

- **Garnishor:** The person or entity who is issuing the garnishment. As officers of the court, attorneys are allowed to issue garnishments directly on behalf of their clients. If you are acting *pro se*, you must have the court issue the garnishment on your behalf, but you will still be considered the garnishor.

Garnishing Bank Accounts

If you (the judgment creditor) happen to know where the judgment debtor has any bank accounts, you can seek to have those garnished. With few exceptions, if a bank has been served with a valid garnishment, they are required to turn over any and all funds of the judgment debtor over to you (up to the amount owed under the judgment). Although there is quite a bit of paperwork involved, the general process of garnishing a bank account is relatively simple. Be sure to check your state's specific laws regarding garnishment procedure.

Garnishing a bank account generally requires that you fill out a writ of garnishment, have it issued by the court (similar to how they issue subpoenas), and then send that writ to the bank along with instructions. Note that you may also be required to send other forms, such as a garnishee response form. You will also likely be required to send a copy of the writ and some type of objection form to the judgment debtor to put them on notice that their bank account has been garnished.

Using Oregon as an example, a judgment creditor would need to send the following documents to the garnishee and the judgment debtor:

**NOTE: The section below should be viewed as an example only!!! If you do not live in Oregon your state's garnishment procedure will likely vary considerably! You must check your state's garnishment laws!*

Documents to be Sent to the Garnishee (ORS 18.650):

- **Writ of Garnishment:** As mentioned above, this is the official order that requires the garnishee to turn over the property.

- **Garnishee Response Form:** This is the form that the garnishee must fill out and return to you, even if they do not hold any property of the judgment debtor.

- **Garnishee Instructions:** These are standard instructions issued to the garnishee.

- **Wage Exemption Calculation Form:** This is the form used by the garnishee to calculate how much of a debtor's wages should be garnished (see the 'GARNISHING WAGES' section below for more information).

- **Search Fee:** If you are sending a writ of garnishment to a bank or other financial institution, you are required to pay them $15 for the trouble of searching their records. A search fee is not required when garnishing a debtor's wages.

Documents to be Sent to the Judgment Debtor (ORS 18.658):

- Writ of Garnishment: Described above.

- Debt Calculation Form: This is the form used to show the debtor exactly how you arrived at the appropriate garnishment amount. You will have to deduct any payments that have been made on the outstanding judgment.

- Notice of Exemptions: This is a list of standard garnishment exemptions that you need to send to the debtor so they know if they have good cause to challenge the garnishment. Examples of exemptions include funds paid as child support, Social Security income, and other government financial assistance

- Challenge to Garnishment Form: This is the form a debtor can use to challenge the garnishment. However, they can only challenge the garnishment if they have good cause to believe the funds in question fall within one of the exemptions. They cannot use this form to challenge the underlying validity of the judgment or the amount awarded.

Although the exact type and name of the forms will vary, your state's garnishment procedure will be similar. Once your particular state's garnishment forms are ready, you will need to take them to the courthouse and present them to the court clerk. You will likely need to pay the court a fee for issuing the writ. The clerk will make sure the writ is complete and then they will ascribe the court's seal to it. Note that some courts may take a few days to approve the writ, in which case they will notify you when it is ready to pick up. Attaching the court's seal makes the writ official and it will have the full authority of the court behind it. Make sure you make at least two copies (and probably a third for your records).

You will then need to mail all of the appropriate forms to the garnishee and the judgment debtor in the manner prescribed by state law.

Unless your state specifically requires you to do so, DO NOT mail the forms to the judgment debtor at the same time that you mail them to the garnishee. If you do, you run the risk of the judgment debtor emptying their bank account before the bank has the chance to seize the funds. Instead, you should wait 7-10 days and then mail them to the judgment debtor. This will give the bank enough time to review your writ and determine if they have any funds subject to garnishment. Most states also require that you hold any funds obtained for a certain number of days before you spend it, in order to give the debtor time to file a challenge to the garnishment.

Garnishing Wages

Garnishing wages works in much the same way as garnishing bank accounts. You will need to fill out all the required forms and send them to the employer and the judgment debtor. Generally, a certain percentage of a judgment debtor's disposable wages will be immune from garnishment. Furthermore, any garnishment that would reduce the judgment debtor's disposable income below a minimum threshold will not be allowed. This means that very low wage earners and/or part time employees may not have sufficient income to be subject to garnishment.

Although there is a lot of paperwork involved, garnishing wages and bank accounts is not difficult. In most cases, the hardest part is finding out whether the judgment creditor has a job and/or where they hold their bank accounts. Do not be discouraged if you are not able to initially collect on your judgment. Money judgments are valid for several years and can often be renewed for an additional amount of time. What's more, money awards usually earn interest at rates much better than most stable investments (in Oregon for example, the interest rate on judgments is 9% per year). Just because the judgment debtor does not have any assets or income now, does not mean they won't be in a better position in a few years. If you sit tight, you will likely be able to collect on your judgment in the future and earn a respectable amount of interest.

CONCLUSION

If you have read this guide you will have a firm understanding of how civil claims proceed in state court. Although we cannot guarantee success, reading this guide will definitely give you an advantage over any opposing party that has not bothered taking similar steps.

Showing the judge you are well prepared and understand how the civil legal system works will give your arguments an air of credibility, especially if your case comes down to believing the testimony of one party over the other. A plaintiff or defendant who shows up unprepared always comes off as less trustworthy, even when their actual claims may have some merit.

Win or lose, you can rest assured that by purchasing this guide and following its advice, you put on a good case. You can hold your head high, knowing that you put on a strong effort based on sound legal theories and a competent understanding of the civil litigation process. Thank you for your purchase and good luck!

APPENDIX 1:
Sample Pleadings

These samples are based on actual pleadings used by the author in the State of Oregon (where he practices law). They are included here to illustrate how such pleadings might look, but the formatting rules of your particular state will vary! We cannot guarantee that using this format to draft your documents will be accepted in other states! Please check your court's formatting rules!

IN THE CIRCUIT COURT FOR THE STATE OF OREGON

FOR THE COUNTY OF CLACKAMAS

JOHN SMITH,	Case No.: 18CV98765
Plaintiff,	**COMPLAINT** (breach of contract)
v.	**CLAIM SUBJECT TO MANDATORY ARBITRATION**
MARK JONES,	
Defendant.	**AMOUNT PRAYED FOR: $5,000**

PLAINTIFF, proceeding *pro se*, brings this Complaint against Defendant and alleges as follows:

1.

At all times material to this Complaint:

-Defendant resided in Clackamas County.

-The events giving rise to this complaint occurred in Clackamas County.

Therefore, jurisdiction in Oregon and this Court is proper, per ORCP 4.

2.

On or around 10/10/2017, Plaintiff and Defendant entered into an oral agreement wherein, Defendant would pay Plaintiff the sum of $7,000 in exchange for Plaintiff painting the outside of Defendant's house. It was agreed that Defendant would provide all the paint and all other materials and the work was to be completed by 12/31/2017. It was further agreed that

COMPLAINT Page 1 of 4

Defendant would pay Plaintiff $2,000 before work began and an additional $5,000 after the work was completed.

3.

On or around 10/20/2017, Defendant paid Plaintiff via personal check the sum of $2,000 in accordance with their agreement. This check was cashed by Plaintiff on 10/21/2017.

4.

Throughout the end of October and November of 2017, Plaintiff painted Defendant's house, per the terms of the agreement. Defendant provided all paint and materials as agreed and the work was completed on or around 11/29/2017. However, when Plaintiff demanded payment of the final $5,000, Defendant refused.

5.

As of the filing of this Complaint, Defendant still has not paid Plaintiff the additional $5,000 that was agreed upon. Plaintiff has attempted to contact Defendant several times regarding this issue, but Defendant has refused to discuss the matter.

FIRST CLAIM FOR RELIEF
(breach of contract)

Plaintiff re-alleges and incorporates Paragraphs 1-5 as if fully set forth here.

6.

Defendant's failure to pay Plaintiff the full $7,000 based on their valid agreement constitutes a material breach of the contract entered into by the parties as described above. Plaintiff has fully performed his obligations under the contract. This breach has caused Plaintiff economic damages in the amount of $5,000.

SECOND CLAIM FOR RELIEF
(unjust enrichment)

Plaintiff re-alleges and incorporates Paragraphs 1-5 as if fully set forth here.

7.

In the alternative, Defendant has been unjustly enriched as a result of the labor Plaintiff expended painting Defendant's house as described above. Defendant has received services from Plaintiff, the reasonable value of which is $7,000, but he has only paid $2,000 for these services. As a result of Defendant's actions, Plaintiff has incurred economic damages in the amount of $5,000.

//
//
//
//
//
//
//
//
//
//
//
//
//
//
//
//

PRAYER FOR RELIEF

8.

WHEREFORE, Plaintiff requests the following relief:

-A money award judgment entered against Defendants for $5,000 in economic damages.

-An award of post-judgment interest on any money damages awarded at a rate of 9% simple per annum.

-Plaintiff's reasonable costs and disbursements for bringing this action.

-Any and all other relief the Court deems just and reasonable under the circumstances.

Dated: 2/01/2018

By: _____
John Smith
123 Lake St.
Oregon City, OR 97045
503-123-4567
email@emailaddress.com

Certificate of Document Preparation.
I certify that (check all boxes and complete all blanks that apply):
A. ☒ I completed this document myself, but I used a template and instructions purchased from a commercial business without receiving any personal legal advice.
B. ☐ I paid or will pay _____ for help in completing and/or reviewing this document.

_____
(Signature)

IN THE CIRCUIT COURT FOR THE STATE OF OREGON
FOR THE COUNTY OF CLACKAMAS

JOHN SMITH,   Case No.: 18CV98765

    Plaintiff,   SUMMONS

    v.

MARK JONES,

    Defendant.

TO: Mark Jones
        987 Phony Ave.
        Canby, OR 97013

NOTICE TO DEFENDANT:

READ THESE PAPERS CAREFULLY!

A lawsuit has been filed against you in the above-mentioned court by John Smith, Plaintiff. Plaintiff's claim is stated in the written Complaint, a copy of which is served upon you with this Summons.

You must appear in this case or Plaintiff will win automatically. To appear, you must file with the court a written legal document called a "motion" or "answer." The motion or answer must be given to the court clerk or administrator within 30 days after the day you were served this Summons, along with the required filing fee. It must be in proper form and have proof of service on the Plaintiff, whose address is below.

//
//
//

SUMMONS Page 1 of 2

If you have any questions, you should contact an attorney immediately. If you need help in finding an attorney, you may contact the Oregon State Bar's Lawyer Referral Service online at www.oregonstatebar.org or by calling (503) 684-3763 (in the Portland metropolitan area) or toll-free elsewhere in Oregon at (800) 452-7636.

Dated: 2/20/2018

                                                      John Smith
                                                      123 Fake St.
                                                      Oregon City, OR 97045
                                                      503-123-4567
                                                      email@emailaddress.com

Certificate of Document Preparation.
I certify that (check all boxes and complete all blanks that apply):
A. ☒ **I completed this document myself, but I used a template and instructions purchased from a commercial business without receiving any personal legal advice.**
B. ☐ **I paid or will pay _____ for help in completing and/or reviewing this document.**

_____
(Signature)

SUMMONS Page 2 of 2

IN THE CIRCUIT COURT FOR THE STATE OF OREGON

FOR THE COUNTY OF CLACKAMAS

SALLY JOHNSON,	Case No.: 18CV13579
Plaintiff,	**ANSWER, AFFIRMATIVE DEFENSES AND COUNTERCLAIMS** (breach of contract/unjust enrichment)
v.	
JAMES WILLIAMS,	**AMOUNT PRAYED FOR: $12,000**
Defendant.	

DEFENDANT, proceeding *pro se*, answers Plaintiff's COMPLAINT and brings COUNTERCLAIMS as follows:

1.

Defendant ADMITS the allegations in Paragraph 1 of the Complaint.

2.

Defendant ADMITS the allegations in Paragraph 2 of the Complaint.

3.

Defendant ADMITS the allegations in Paragraph 3 of the Complaint.

4.

Regarding Paragraph 4 of the Complaint, Defendant ADMITS that he did not pay the additional $10,000, but DENIES the allegation that such amount is still due.

5.

Regarding Paragraphs 5, 6, and 7 of the Complaint, Defendant DENIES that Plaintiff is

ANSWER, AFFIRMATIVE DEFENSES AND COUNTERCLAIM Page 1 of 4

entitled to any of the relief claimed.

AFFIRMATIVE DEFENSES

6.

Defendant asserts the following affirmative defenses.

-Lack of consideration: Plaintiff's loan to Defendant should be considered a gift as Defendant did not offer any consideration for the initial loan.

-Accord and Satisfaction: Plaintiff agreed to cancel the remaining amount owed under the initial agreement in exchange for Defendant's work on her property.

FIRST COUNTERCLAIM
(breach of contract)

7.

Defendant alleges the following Counterclaim against Defendant:

Defendant admits that he stopped making $500 monthly payments to Plaintiff around September of 2015. This is because Plaintiff and Defendant entered into an oral agreement a few months earlier, the terms of which involved Plaintiff cancelling the remaining debt owed by Defendant (after he made payments through September of 2015). In exchange, Defendant agreed to perform yardwork and maintenance around Defendant's property for the next three years, whenever it was reasonably requested by Plaintiff (Plaintiff is elderly and cannot perform this work herself). It was further agreed that after the first two years of performing this work, Defendant would then pay Plaintiff $10 per hour for all work performed (in addition to cancelling the remaining debt from the original agreement).

8.

For approximately one year (from 8/2015-9/2016), Defendant routinely performed yardwork/maintenance for Plaintiff, including: mowing the lawn on a regular basis, changing the brakes on Plaintiff's car, assisting in replacing the roof on Plaintiff's house, and clearing brush from the property. In total, Defendant performed 400 hours of work on Plaintiff's behalf.

9.

For reasons unknown to Defendant, during the fall of 2016, Plaintiff told Defendant not to do any more yard work and demanded that he pay her back the $10,000 that was supposed to be cancelled. Defendant would have performed an additional 400 hours of work on Plaintiff's behalf under the terms of the new contract if Plaintiff had not breached it.

10.

Plaintiff's actions as described above have caused Defendant $12,000 in economic damages, representing:

-$6,000 for the reasonable value of Defendant's labor (at $15/hr) for the 400 hours of work he performed from 9/2015-9/2016; and

-$6,000 for the reasonable value of Defendant's labor (at $15/hr), that he would have continued to perform under the new contract.

SECOND COUNTERCLAIM
(unjust enrichment)

11.

Defendant alleges the following Counterclaim against Defendant:

Plaintiff has received the material benefit of the work performed by Defendant, as described above, without offering any just compensation.

12.

Plaintiff's actions as described above have caused Defendant $6,000 in economic damages, representing:

-$6,000 for the reasonable value of Defendant's labor (at $15/hr) for the 400 hours of work he

ANSWER, AFFIRMATIVE DEFENSES AND COUNTERCLAIM Page 3 of 4

performed from 9/2015-9/2016; and

PRAYER FOR RELIEF

13.

WHEREFORE, Defendant requests the following relief:

-Dismissal of all of Plaintiff's claims with prejudice.

-A money award entered against Plaintiff for $12,000 in economic damages.

-An award of Defendant's reasonable costs and disbursements for defending this action.

-An award of post-judgment interest on any money damages awarded at a rate of 9% simple per annum.

-Any and all other relief the Court deems just and reasonable under the circumstances.

Dated: 2/28/18

By: _____
James Williams
987 Phony Ave.
Canby, OR 97013
503-987-6543
email@emailaddress.com

Certificate of Document Preparation.
I certify that (check all boxes and complete all blanks that apply):
A. ☐ I completed this document myself, but I used a template and instructions purchased from a commercial business without receiving any personal legal advice.
B. ☐ I paid or will pay _____ for help in completing and/or reviewing this document.

_____
(Signature)

ANSWER, AFFIRMATIVE DEFENSES AND COUNTERCLAIM Page 4 of 4

IN THE CIRCUIT COURT FOR THE STATE OF OREGON

FOR THE COUNTY OF CLACKAMAS

JOHN SMITH,	Case No.: 18CV98765
Plaintiff,	PLAINTIFF'S FIRST REQUEST FOR PRODUCTION OF DOCUMENTS
v.	
MARK JONES,	
Defendant.	

TO: **Mark Jones, Defendant**
987 Phony Ave.
Canby, OR 97013

Plaintiff requests that Defendant respond to the following Request for Production of Documents pursuant to ORCP 36(B) and 43, and that the responses be served on Plaintiff 30 days after service at the following address: John Smith, 123 Fake St., Oregon City, OR 97045. The documents shall be grouped and labeled with a designation of the request to which they are responsive and (whenever possible) submitted in electronic PDF format.

DEFINITIONS

1. The term "documents" includes any and all notes (handwritten or typed), memoranda, correspondence and other writings, drawings, graphs, charts, photographs, phonorecords, audio tapes, videotapes, computerized records, electronic data (including e-mails) and other data

PLAINTIFF'S FIRST REQUEST FOR PRODUCTION OF DOCUMENTS Page 1 of 4

compilations from which information can be obtained, and translated, if necessary, by the Plaintiff through detection devices into reasonably usable form.

2. The term "person" includes not only natural persons, but corporations, unincorporated associations, or any other entity, as well as employees and agents of the foregoing, and shall be comprehensive, whether used in the plural or singular form.

3. The phrase "relating to or evidencing" shall mean in any way, directly or indirectly concerning, constituting, considering, modifying, amending, confirming, endorsing, representing, supporting, qualifying, terminating, revoking, canceling, derived from, based upon or negating.

4. The terms "and" and "or" shall be construed either disjunctively or conjunctively as necessary to bring within the scope of this request any documents or objects which might otherwise be construed to be outside its scope.

5. When used herein, "identify" means to describe with particularity. When referring to a person, "identify" means to state the person's full name, address, telephone and any other contact information. When referring to a document, "identify" means to describe the document by author, date, content and identifying mark (such as Bates number). When referring to a statute, policy, or rule, "identify" means to state the statute, policy or rule by number or title. For anything else, "identify" means to provide sufficient information to allow the reader to understand the response and follow up on the information.

REQUEST FOR PRODUCTION NO. 1: All documents (including, but not limited to, text messages and emails) in which Defendant discusses the painting of his house by Defendant that took place during October and November of 2017.

RESPONSE:

REQUEST FOR PRODUCTION NO. 2: All documents (including, but not limited to, text messages and emails) in which Defendant discusses the painting of his house by anyone other than Defendant from 1/01/2017 through the present.

RESPONSE:

REQUEST FOR PRODUCTION NO. 3: Any documents that relate to the payment of $2,000 via personal check that was made by Defendant to Plaintiff on or around 10/20/2017, including (but not limited to), a copy of the personal check, a copy of any check receipt or register that shows the payment was made, and a copy of Defendant's bank statement that shows the check was cashed.

RESPONSE:

REQUEST FOR PRODUCTION NO. 4: All documents relating to any other solicitations or requests for bids that were sought by Defendant relating to the painting of his house from 1/1/2017 though the present.

RESPONSE:

//

//

//

//

REQUEST FOR PRODUCTION NO. 5: All receipts that relate to any painting materials that were used in the painting of Defendant's house that took place during October and November of 2017.

RESPONSE:

Dated: 2/01/2018   By: _____
                             John Smith
                             123 Fake St.
                             Oregon City, OR 97045
                             503-123-4567
                             email@emailaddress.com

IN THE CIRCUIT COURT FOR THE STATE OF OREGON
FOR THE COUNTY OF CLACKAMAS

JOHN SMITH,	Case No.: 18CV98765
Plaintiff,	CIVIL SUBPOENA
v.	
MARK JONES,	
Defendant.	

STATE OF OREGON)
) ss.
County of Clackamas)

IN THE NAME OF THE STATE OF OREGON

TO: **FRANK JONES**

You are hereby commanded to appear in the Circuit Court for the County of Clackamas, at the Courthouse at 807 Main St., Oregon City, OR 97045 on the 15th day of March, 2018, at 1:30pm to give evidence in the above cause on behalf of Plaintiff.

Witness my hand and the seal of said Court affixed in _____ this _____ day of _____, 20____.
By: _____

I hereby certify that I, on _____/_____/_____ in said county and state served the within subpoena on the within named person by delivering a copy thereof to said person (witness), personally and in person, and offering or giving the witness the required fees he or she is entitled to for travel and one day's attendance.

Dated: _____

Jane Williams
55 Main St.
Oregon City, OR 97045
503-111-2222

CIVIL SUBPOENA Page 1 of 1

IN THE CIRCUIT COURT FOR THE STATE OF OREGON

FOR THE COUNTY OF CLACKAMAS

JOHN SMITH,	Case No.: 18CV98765
Plaintiff,	PLAINTIFF'S MOTION TO COMPEL PRODUCTION OF DOCUMENTS
v.	ORCP 46
MARK JONES,	ORAL ARGUMENT REQUESTED
Defendant.	

1.

UTCR 5.010 INFORMATION

Plaintiff attempted to resolve this issue with Defendant before filing this motion. The parties conferred via telephone on 1/31/2018, but were unable to resolve this issue.

2.

UTCR 5.050 INFORMATION

Plaintiff requests oral argument on this motion. The time estimated for oral argument is approximately 30 minutes. Court reporting services are requested.

3.

MOTION

Pursuant to ORCP 46, Plaintiff moves the Court for an Order compelling production of the following documents:

PLAINTIFF'S MOTION TO COMPEL PRODUCTION OF DOCUMENTS
Page 1 of 2

1. All text messages relating to Plaintiff's painting of Defendant's house in October and November of 2017.

These documents were requested in Plaintiff's First Request for Production of Documents, which was sent to Defendant on 2/1/2018. Exhibit 1. They are relevant to the case at hand as the allegations in Plaintiff's complaint allege a breach of contract, the terms of which may be revealed in the requested text messages. This request is not overly burdensome and it is likely to lead to admissible evidence.

4.

This motion is further supported by the *Declaration of John Smith in Support of Plaintiff's Motion to Compel Production of Documents*.

Dated: 4/01/2018

By: _____
John Smith
123 Fake St.
Oregon City, OR 97045
503-123-4567
email@emailaddress.com

Certificate of Document Preparation.
I certify that (check all boxes and complete all blanks that apply):
A. ☒ **I completed this document myself, but I used a template and instructions purchased from a commercial business without receiving any personal legal advice.**
B. ☐ **I paid or will pay** _____ **for help in completing and/or reviewing this document.**

_____
(Signature)

PLAINTIFF'S MOTION TO COMPEL PRODUCTION OF DOCUMENTS

IN THE CIRCUIT COURT FOR THE STATE OF OREGON

FOR THE COUNTY OF CLACKAMAS

JOHN SMITH,	Case No.: 18CV98765
Plaintiff,	DEFENDANT'S RESPONSE TO PLAINTIFF'S MOTION FOR SUMMARY JUDGMENT
v.	
MARK JONES,	ORCP 47
Defendant.	ORAL ARGUMENT REQUESTED

1.

UTCR 5.050 INFORMATION

Defendant requests oral argument on this motion. The time estimated for oral argument is approximately 30 minutes. Court reporting services are requested.

2.

CASE SUMMARY

Defendant agrees with the case summary as cited by Plaintiff, except for the following:

1. $7,000 was never the agreed upon final price.

3.

UNDISPUTED MATERIAL FACTS

Defendant also agrees with the undisputed facts cited in Plaintiff's motion except for the following:

DEFENDANT'S RESPONSE TO PLAINTIFF'S MOTION FOR SUMMARY JUDGMENT
Page 1 of 4

1. Defendant never agreed that the final price for the house painting was to be $7,000. The text messages contained in Exhibit 3 are merely negotiations and do not represent a final agreement on contract terms. Plaintiff's conclusions to the contrary are merely his interpretation of the facts.

4.

STANDARD FOR SUMMARY JUDGMENT

Summary judgment is proper if:

> "The pleadings, depositions, affidavits, declarations, and admissions on file show that there is no genuine issue as to any material fact and that the moving party is entitled to prevail as a matter of law. No genuine issue as to a material fact exists if, based on the record before the court viewed in a manner most favorable to the adverse party, no objectively reasonable juror could return a verdict for the adverse party on the matter that is the subject of the motion for summary judgment." ORCP 47.

As explained below, there is indeed a genuine issue of material fact relating to some of the elements of Plaintiff's claims.

5.

ARGUMENT

Claim One: Breach of Contract:

Defendant admits that he and Plaintiff had an agreement for Plaintiff to paint Defendant's house. Defendant further admits he paid Plaintiff $2,000 on 10/20/2017 as part of this agreement. However, that was to be the final price. Initially, Plaintiff wanted $5,000 more and Defendant did consider that at one point (as reflected in Exhibit 3 of Plaintiff's Motion for Summary Judgment). However, ultimately it was decided that $2,000 would be the only amount paid for the house. See *Declaration of Mark Jones in Support of Defendant's Response* (filed

DEFENDANT'S RESPONSE TO PLAINTIFF'S MOTION FOR SUMMARY JUDGMENT
Page 2 of 4

concurrently herewith). Defendant complied with all of his obligations under the contract and does not owe Plaintiff any additional amounts.

Claim Two: Unjust Enrichment:

Since Defendant has paid Plaintiff in accordance with the terms of their agreement, Plaintiff's unjust enrichment claim must also fail. Defendant has not received any unjust benefit. In the alternative, even if Plaintiff does have a valid unjust enrichment claim, there is a genuine issue of material fact as to how much he has been enriched. Defendant's alleged unjust enrichment can only be determined by evaluating evidence of what a fair price for painting a house should be in this community. Furthermore, Defendant will submit evidence at trial that the poor quality of Plaintiff's work does not warrant any further payments, even if other people might charge more for painting houses. In other words, the fair value of Plaintiff's work is (at a maximum) $2,000, which has already been paid. In any case, there is no evidence in the record regarding the fair market value of Plaintiff's work. Even if there were, there would be a genuine issue of material fact as to whether or not any such evidence was accurate.

//
//
//
//
//
//
//
//
//

DEFENDANT'S RESPONSE TO PLAINTIFF'S MOTION FOR SUMMARY JUDGMENT

6.

CONCLUSION

As explained above, there are genuine issues of material fact as to what the final price of the house painting job was supposed to be and regarding what is the fair value of the house painting job. Since the evidence must be weighed in the light most favorable to the non-moving party, the Court should deny Plaintiff's motion in its entirety.

Dated: 4/22/2018   By: _____
                                Mark Jones
                                987 Phony Ave.
                                Canby, OR 97013
                                503-987-6543
                                email@emailaddress.com

Certificate of Document Preparation.
I certify that (check all boxes and complete all blanks that apply):
A. ☒ I completed this document myself, but I used a template and instructions purchased from a commercial business without receiving any personal legal advice.
B. ☐ I paid or will pay _____ for help in completing and/or reviewing this document.

_____
(Signature)

DEFENDANT'S RESPONSE TO PLAINTIFF'S MOTION FOR SUMMARY JUDGMENT

APPENDIX 2:
Glossary

AFFIRMATIVE DEFENSE: A type of defense asserted in a defendant's answer in which, even if the allegations in the plaintiff's complaint are true, the plaintiff is still not entitled to relief. For example, if the allegations in the complaint are true, but the statute of limitations has expired, the defendant would assert the affirmative defense of failure to bring a claim within the statutory period.

ANSWER: The formal reply to a complaint, filed by the defendant. An answer will usually deny the claims made in the complaint and/or will otherwise assert how the plaintiff is not entitled to any of the relief sought.

APPEAL: A request for a higher court to review the decision of a lower court. Appeals are not allowed in every instance. There must be a specific reason (specified by the courts or state law) that allows an appeal. For example, if a judge excludes evidence and you object, you could appeal asking for a new trial. But if a jury simply decides against you because they found the other party more convincing, you generally cannot appeal.

ARBITRATION: A less formal, but usually binding, proceeding in which a civil dispute is resolved by a private arbitrator, rather than a judge. In many cases, arbitration is mandatory.

BENCH TRIAL: A trial in which there is no jury. The judge will decide all issues of law and fact.

CERTIFICATE OF SERVICE: A document filed with the court showing that service has been completed in accordance with the rules of civil procedure.

CLAIM FOR RELIEF: A specific cause of action alleged in a complaint, such as a claim of negligence or a claim of racial discrimination.

COMPLAINT: The initial document filed by a plaintiff that begins a civil lawsuit. It is a statement of how the plaintiff has been wronged by the defendant, why they should be compensated, and how much compensation they believe is warranted. It includes one or more claims for relief and alleges how each element of that claim has been satisfied.

CONTEMPT OF COURT: The offense of disobeying a court order. A judge can find a person in contempt and impose sanctions (usually a fine or other civil penalty, but on rare occasions it can include incarceration). In addition, if a party believes someone else is disobeying an order, they can ask the judge to find that person in contempt by filing a motion.

CONTRACT: Any agreement (oral or written), in which an offer has been made by one party, accepted by another, and some consideration has been given (such as money, or performance of a specific task). Breach of contract is one of the most commonly filed civil claims (whether in small claims court or regular, circuit court).

CONTRACT LAW: One of two broad categories of civil lawsuits. All legal issues dealing with any written or oral agreement will be based on contract law.

DECLARATION: A written statement made under oath, usually attached to a motion or other pleading to support the arguments contained therein. A declaration can be made by a party or anyone else who has personal knowledge that is relevant to the case.

DEFAULT JUDGMENT: A judgment entered against a defendant who has failed to appear after being properly served with a summons and complaint.

DEFENDANT: A person who has been accused of wrongdoing in civil court in the form of a complaint being filed against them.

DEPONENT: The witness who is being deposed.

DEPOSITION: A formal interview of a witness that is recorded (usually by a court reporter transcribing the deposition).

DISCOVERY: The stage of a civil lawsuit wherein both parties are obligated to turn over any potential evidence that is relevant to a claim or defense.

DISMISSAL WITHOUT PREJUDICE: The dismissal of a plaintiff's case wherein they can refile their complaint. In other words, a judge thought the case had serious flaws, but the flaws could potentially be resolved and the case could still be refiled if the deficiencies are corrected.

DISMISSAL WITH PREJUDICE: The dismissal of a plaintiff's case, wherein the plaintiff cannot refile against the defendant regarding the same issue. The judge has decided that the problems with the case are so great, they cannot possibly be corrected.

ELEMENT: A specific aspect of a claim that must be properly alleged (and ultimately proven) to prevail on a claim for relief. A claim will normally have several elements, each of which must be proven by a preponderance of the evidence.

EVIDENCE: Anything that is submitted in a court proceeding to prove or disprove any claim or defense. Evidence includes (but is not limited to) oral testimony of witnesses, documents, video recordings, and material objects.

EXHIBIT: Any piece of evidence (other than witness testimony) that is submitted for review in a court proceeding, whether at trial or pursuant to a motion, deposition or other hearing.

GARNISHMENT: The legal seizing of another person's property (such as wages or funds in a bank account). Garnishment is often instituted to collect money awarded in a judgment.

HEARING: A proceeding before a judge in which evidence is presented and a decision is made. The decision at a hearing may affect one aspect of a case, or it may resolve the case entirely, depending on the nature of the specific hearing.

INTERROGATORIES: A formal request issued by a party during discovery in which they ask the other party to answer a list of questions in writing.

JUDGMENT CREDITOR: A person who has been awarded monetary damages in a civil lawsuit.

JUDGMENT DEBTOR: A person who has been ordered to pay monetary damages in a civil lawsuit.

JURY TRIAL: A trial in which a jury decides all factual issues. A judge will preside over the case and decide all legal issues, but the final decision regarding liability and damages will be made by the jury.

LOCAL RULES: Specific rules put in place by county courts. All proceedings in these particular counties must follow their local rules.

MEDIATION: A formal meeting between the parties and a neutral mediator in which the mediator attempts to broker a settlement that is agreeable to both sides. Unlike an arbitrator, the mediator does not have any authority to issue a decision in favor of one party. Their only purpose is to negotiate with both parties and attempt to craft a mutually agreeable settlement. In some instances, parties are required to attend a mediation session and work towards resolving the issue in good faith.

MOTION: Any formal request by a party, asking the court to take a certain course of action.

MOTION FOR SUMMARY JUDGMENT: A formal request by either party asking the judge to find in their favor without going to trial. A party files a motion for summary judgment when they believe there are no material issues of fact that need to be considered in a trial. For example, if a plaintiff in a deposition admits that a specific element of a claim never actually occurred, the defendant may move for summary judgment because there is no dispute about the existence of that specific element of the claim.

MOTION TO COMPEL: A formal request by either party to force the other party to produce certain documents or answer certain questions. Such a motion would be filed after a party asks for the information, but the other side has refused to provide it. At this point the party ordered to produce the information can be found in contempt if the motion is granted and they still refuse to produce the documents or answer the questions.

MOTION TO DISMISS: A formal request by a defendant to dismiss one or more of plaintiff's claims. Usually due to the plaintiff failing to properly allege a cause of action.

OBJECTION: A formal protest by one party to the actions of the other party. For example, if a party seeks to submit evidence that is not in accordance with a state's rules of evidence, a party might object to its entry on the grounds that it fails to comply with a specific rule. Alternatively, if a party tries to ask a witness a question, the answer to which would not be admissible, the opposing party should object to the question before the witness answers.

ORAL ARGUMENT: Appearances by both parties (usually in relation to a filed motion) to argue their points personally in front of a judge before the judge makes a decision regarding the motion. Oral argument is held after a motion, response, and reply have all been filed.

PARTY: A plaintiff or defendant in a civil case.

PLAINTIFF: A person who files a civil lawsuit against a defendant.

PLEADING (noun): Any formal document that is filed with the court in a civil case.

PREJUDICIAL: In this context, prejudicial refers to how *unfairly* harmful a piece of evidence is. Evidence that would not be excluded for any other reason, can still be excluded if it will unfairly bias a jury. For example, if the jury knows a party has been convicted of a crime unrelated to the issue at hand, that could unfairly skew their impression of the party. The party could seek to have that fact excluded as having more prejudicial than probative value.

PROBATIVE: A term used to describe how strong a piece of evidence is in regards to its ability to help prove or disprove any claim or defense. How probative a piece of evidence is will often be a factor in whether or not it is admitted into the record. Evidence that has no probative value will likely be excluded.

PROCESS SERVER: A person who is hired by a party to deliver legal documents to persons in accordance with the rules of civil procedure.

PRO SE: Latin phrase meaning, "for oneself". It refers to any plaintiff or defendant that does not have an attorney. They are referred to as a *pro se* litigant or proceeding *pro se*.

REPLY: A reply to a party's response to a motion (filed by the party who originally filed the motion).

REQUEST FOR ADMISSIONS (RFA): A formal request issued by a party during discovery in which they ask the opposing party to admit or deny specific facts about the case.

REQUEST FOR PRODUCTION (RFP): A formal request issued by a party during discovery in which they ask for all potential evidence (usually in the form of written documents) that is relevant to any claim or defense in a civil case.

RESPONSE: A response to a motion filed by the opposing party.

RULES OF CIVIL PROCEDURE: The basic rules of civil court proceedings. Each state will have their own set of civil procedure rules (the official name of these rules will vary from state to state).

SERVICE: The term used to refer to specific notice that pleadings have been received by an opposing party.

SMALL CLAIMS COURT: A division of a state court that handles claims of low economic value (the exact amount varies by state). In most states, attorneys are not allowed to represent parties in small claims court. It is intended to be a less formal and more cost-effective venue for resolving civil disputes.

STATUTE OF LIMITATIONS: A period set by law in which a claim for relief must be filed. For example, if the statute of limitations on a personal injury (negligence) case is two years, the plaintiff would need to file a claim for negligence within two years of the date they discovered the injury.

STATUTES: The codified laws of a state. The official name of these statutes will vary from state to state.

SUBPOENA: A command by a court or attorney requiring a person to appear for a deposition or hearing/trial.

SUBPOENA DUCES TECUM: A command by a court or attorney requiring a person to produce specific documents or other material objects.

SUMMONS: A command to appear and defend oneself in a civil lawsuit. Served with a complaint. Failure to appear can result in a default judgment being entered against the defendant.

TORT LAW: The other broad category of civil lawsuits that basically includes any type of wrongful act committed by another (other than breach of contract cases), such as battery or negligence.

TRIAL: A proceeding in which a final decision is made based on the merits of a case. A hearing where evidence is presented and a judge or jury finds in favor of the plaintiff or defendant.

TRIAL COURT RULES: More specific rules of a state that govern courtroom procedure which all county courts must follow.

WITNESS: Any person that provides testimony in a court proceeding. They can be a party to the litigation or any other person.

www.ingramcontent.com/pod-product-compliance
Lightning Source LLC
Chambersburg PA
CBHW082249220526
45469CB00009B/2934